Human Self-development. Basics.

Lecture

Love

&

Life

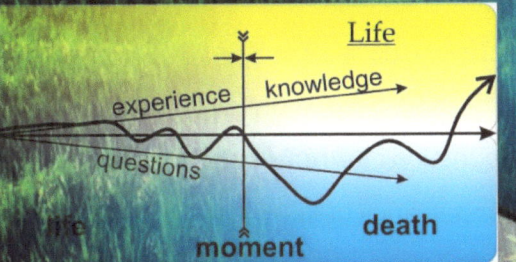

The system of collected facts about the content and possibility of human life. Love, respect and understanding are formed and form the quantity of human life.

2015

Content

Description

Lecture "Human Self-development. Basics."
The lecture is theoretically practical information. Its aim is to encourage the person to a more conscious understanding of the personal and environmental life. The lecture demonstrates knowledge of understanding of the human life's components, the meaning of development and self-development. The system shows you the basics of human life. Depending on the experience of the person, this lecture will remain unknown as death and life, or will give a boost to self-responsibility of understanding of his life in the surrounding life.

The system of collected facts about the content and possibility of human life. Love, respect and understanding are formed and form the quantity of human life.

About the Book
The book reflects the results of studies of more than 15 years. Areas of research are the psychology of life in general and human life through his body physiology, psychology, soul, energy, human rights and peace, content protection and rights, yoga, nutrition, healthy lifestyle, business, the issue of self-development. Research continues. The purpose of the book is to ask a human to live with understanding, consciousness or in chaos, and invite everyone to join. The purpose of research - life through love, respect and understanding in the practical usage and database creation of experience for documentation and to transfer information to other people and to future generations.

About the Author
The author explores the life from a childhood. He began to think of writing books in ninth grade. What am I going to write when I do not know anything? I can write something, but it will not make sense. Since then he began research work on the study of human life. The author has experience as a teacher of foreign languages, translator of foreign languages, sales manager, businessman, he practiced psychological counseling, massage, yoga, energy, a diary writing, articles, poems and small stories writing. Author explored various spheres of human activity and behavior parallel. All it took more than 15 years of life.

Author: Mykola V.
Ukraine , 2015

Lecture. Human self-development. Basics.

Foreword

Project VM Love And Life appeared after the year 2000. Then it was only its name without understanding the details of its content, but the general sense is concerned in the word "love", the connecting part "and" and the word "life." They gave understanding of the direction of thinking – to live with love to life.

My name is Mykola. My personality should not be the center of the lecture. The center of the narrative become words, their meaning, communication between the content of the words and the overall guiding objective. Everything has its value, time and purpose. We are like people who have the capacity to understand but not always realize it. That's it and should be that way. The flower grows when the environment needs it under certain circumstances. It quickly begins its life finding the way through the soil and various obstacles. A delicate flower can pass through the asphalt stubbornly and persistently making its way through difficulties. And this is a flower, not even a child, the human child, which has its opportunities and environment for life. However, this flower or better to say life in the form of the flower creates its way. It just makes its way to the goal of creating a new life. Life does not doubt and does not thinks. It searches desired possibilities and necessary tools for self-realization. The flower has its own content and its purpose for the manifestation of the necessities of life. Everything has its purpose, which makes it an intermediary chain between needs and results. And it's only a matter of the flower, which can be cut and it seems that life should go, too. It is, but life does not consist of a single flower and is a huge system of planned or rather orderly life of all its components in order to develop itself. Life progresses all this through various stages of experience with time. Flower grows up. It's not in a hurry and is growing freely at the same time despite how much time it requires. It grows, overcomes difficulties and achieves its development's stages.

Only a man has opportunities to see such detail as time and his capabilities over time. A person may notice and does it a lot. To a greater extent, he develops opportunities of the vision. Like being in the dark he gets used to seeing objects closely first and farther, and farther. He begins to open such opportunities gradually more and more, and even to create different knowledge in various fields. This happens gradually, gathering knowledge to each other and constantly forming a whole library of facts. Man uses them, experimenting and exploring. He begins to understand the significance of the facts, and how they work with each other, and which results they give. Like math exercises at school. But there are mainly readymade data at school, which you need to know how to use them in a certain order to find a solution and to check the exercise's task, and to find mistakes in your actions. That trains well skills to sum up numbers and task, and to find new solutions. It remains only to use them more often in daily life. When it doesn't happen the person loses awareness of the value of the obtained skills and their usefulness. Loss of communication is important for understanding the meaning of any steps, thoughts direction and results as meaning.

I didn't understand the project well. It was not even a project at the beginning of its name creation, which was just the name of my e-mail address. Once applying for a job an employer noted that my e-mail had a beautiful name. Then I was asked what I wanted from life. These questions were put me at first and I was in good mood to say 'I need to help other people to see their lives happier'. As a result life must go to understanding and results, anyway we are on that way. There are a lot of ways and variants, too. Knowledge can help and confuse at the same time. Aiming means the way, which is formed gradually with the development of new opportunities, resources and needs, respectively. Thus was forming the understanding of these words "love and life" in everyday life, common names of common meanings that we can see and use every day at work, at home, on vacation, in relationships, in the journey, and so on. Actions repeat and give us more examples to understand their common meaning. If we speak different languages, it does not mean that we can not say the same idea in different languages!

Thus a man collected different experience and a different understanding of life, from different sides about the same - life. This meaning is continuing to add additional facts and additions, and explaining meanings. Such way formed the feeling, meaning and understanding of love, its forms and examples. Their depth and connection to various spheres of manifestation. After all, people love animals, expensive thing, a mother, another person, life, reading and writing, and feelings, it all just add the range of manifestations and spheres of use for better understanding of the power of love, its width and depth. In recent years, after 2010, I began to understand the purpose of the word "and" in a general meaning of these three words "love and life". "I" complements and binds these words for a better understanding of life in these two complementary key details.

Love and Life as the action and the feeling created a man. You can understand the significance of these things only after years of life. Years of life and love, good and bad actions, different experience with bad and pleasant sensations. All this inspires us as people to various actions and once again we are moving in a circle of different actions and feelings. We call this life and we love it for the gained experience, sure, if we have understood why it happened. And if we had not figured out, then we got a sense of disappointment and unpleasant experience. It hasn't made us a good foundation, but mistrust and caution. It can be even much worse when we accept things as they are and do not want to find out what was wrong. We just blame someone and try to pour all the pain out on someone else. All we just destroy and do it subconsciously, because our actions are on emotions and we want to show them up. Our own actions show it doesn't give proper results and again we try to understand until we do things, that can strongly knock us out of the looped state in which we find ourselves.

The looped state, fanaticism and emotions take place and have the limits, which everybody has different. It all depends on how much it can hurt us personally or others, and most important - how we are aware of what we are doing and why. This understanding does not come all at once, and even often ever. But even to stop and get out of this state is the hardest thing and it takes a lot of time. It is so alike alcoholism, drugs, obesity, and a sense of loss in life.

Different experience for example at work gives us the opportunity to learn better to understand our own actions and responsibility. This is our discipline. Especially because we have reasons to fear that holds us, as the fear of being fired, money loss, of losing the stimulus and the value of our life in doings and its meaning. Work helps to get the sense of life in what we do. The work takes away our personality and develops feeling of virtual life, that we can assume as real. Such things can happen and always take place when a person forgets about himself and does not improve himself. Then we get the main question "what does it mean to improve yourself"? It creates confusion and misunderstanding. And it doesn't mean if you have money or not. At work we understand the sequence and have stimulus that we don't have for our own lives and soul, but fear and no one pays us for our own self-development. It looks like true and even not. Stimulus exists, it may be the fear of death, poverty and frustration, and of other things, which we are afraid of and do not want to have it in our life. But only they can encourage us to move into the unknown. Each step makes us wonder where we are going and why. And every other moment can hide the answers. All it looks confusing and unclear. Though it also makes sense, because only a man can find so many questions, information and experience that can confuse us and make us at a loss, and this, too, anyway has the answers to get out of this situation!

Misunderstanding, confusion, uncertainty, failure or inability to find your way and purpose in life as well as the purpose of life itself are important questions for people with similar issues. Most important is that we have questions and people, too. If we have it all, the rest is only to determine all the components. Yes and we need to treat this as a task. When we make main questions or just first few ones it will be the point to start understand and search the answers.

Such information of gathering and processing helps us to develop an understanding of the system of knowledge about life. Yes, it is the whole system with many details and examples to form a systematic understanding and formation of thinking in a certain direction - understanding. That understanding allows to know and realize what you're dealing with and what to do.

It is worth remembering the diversity of experience in various fields. It looks more as repeating of what was said but only the repetition of the same things in different areas allows us to emphasize the importance of the experience.

Experience as a word became to have more meaningful content in detail. All has its purpose or you can create it. Something always is pushing ahead the following. When a man needs to go to a toilet, because he's got a lot of accumulated fluid in the body, a man feels this need and runs to the destination. A very short and valuable example for understanding the basic principles of life. And this is only the basis of the principles required. As the alphabet, without which we simply can not read what is written with the alphabet.

Alphabet and the ability to read encourage us to other great deeds. Accumulation of information creates a different scope of its ownership. It looks like different kinds of business or just different things that a person needs for life and its self-development, which are necessary for everybody in general. So learning to read, we begin to read. Next questions come what to do with the knowledge and what is it for?! And from this point begins interesting, because it's not so easy to understand it at once. It doesn't look so simple. Why do we read fiction books? Do we need it to enrich our vocabulary and the ability to speak better!? Yes, but that's not all. Does it mean more opportunities?! Yes, and it is for sure. Otherwise what am I writing and why? But all this stuff written here has its own meaning, consistent presentation of thoughts, different parts and small goals, big goals and one or more principal ones. Everything makes sense, but it turns out that the ability to read does not give us confidence that we can understand the meaning attached. Why is this happening?! Every next time we read a book, we begin to understand it better in these words that we read for the umpteenth time. Maybe we just were not interested in that sense and we wanted to know some other knowledge to understand it or even just for fun?! Actually it is, so everyone can and will understand only what he can realize and what he wishes. I will repeat such things sometimes for a better understanding, which are being formed. Thinking can aligned how a stick or a sword can be aligned too, or anything else. It can be hard to imagine, but if you think a little about the text, it is possible to rewrite it or add, find errors and so on. Such thing a man can do or it can be done with him. He is like a content that can complemented, erased and modified.

Aiming to find such items you can find people and opportunities to see different things of psychological moment, the types of relationship and person's thoughts. Communicating you can start to see how a person thinks and in what direction. Probably everyone has heard from the movies, that every person's word can be used against him. For the formation of consciousness on a conscious level you need to use his words as a reflected fact of the thoughts and the ability to adjust it.

Communication has perhaps the greatest power and influence on the person, of course it depends on the person. It gives the greatest experience in the formation of thinking, of his own or someone else's. This creates an important experience, one among the various spheres of human activity. What is a man's interest in it? Actually, it's not the right question. Because communication and the use of communication are the major means of forming thinking and thinking facts, as to the experience of operated information and abstract play of imagination. If you use the energy impact on a person without speech, everything happens more slowly and the man becomes worse. It scares her because she did not understand what was happening. Therefore, each person can be applied better to use tools of its level. As well as to communicate in English with someone who speaks Russian. You can not explain. If you speak the same language, everything will be much easier to understand.

Therefore, time is going on and experience in different spheres, different work, communication with people, work with information, physical work with human body, various experiments in communication and behavior with other people, various relations, feelings, love, household work and many, many other examples and variants, all it completes the picture of understanding and opportunities to see the unknown. After all, once I personally found out and saw that everything is just around us and even within us. We just do not know how to read it, someone does not know the alphabet, someone can not and does not want to read, and someone has other reasons. And all around us is in the open state. I will repeat it sometimes for better understanding. I like when teachers of romano-germanic filology in the university often say a proverb "repetition is the mother of learning". I like another one "Experience is the best teacher"

You gather experience to the point when there is no way but share it because it changed you a long time ago and people around you look like a bit different. You can see their needs and their thinking, and you realize that this knowledge can be useful for them. This information is being tested all the time in different areas and on different people. Amounts of information only increase, as well as their quality. The most important point is the quality.

Applying for a job, I met a colleague and he asked me about the business organization. I was interested more in information business and the ability to provide trainings, education. It inspired me to develop themes for lectures and a beginning one. It is the basis because since the beginning the lecture is to help chose your conscious lifestyle choice. This will be discussed. Between realizing the bases and beginning of a conscious choice, there is plenty of time, and for each person it is different, as there may be no choice at all when selecting a different direction.

Therefore, the lecture is ready and it remains just to retell it. The Lecture now is one with prepared questions. It is the basic and most important. I realized this after I started doing drawings and red it for my companion individually. Pictures explain everything.

Such a lecture is the only. Topics for research and therefore for future lectures are recorded. You can complement and even cancel. I need to see needs of people in collaborative research or interest. I developed questions and I can tell you all the experience for creating new knowledge and its quantity.

The lecture needs a hall, chairs, whiteboard and pen, projector and audio sound.

1- Beginning and preparing for the lecture

A Greeting

Everybody is welcome for the lecture "Human self-development. The Basics."! Please take your seats, we are starting. Who is late, just find a place and welcome)).

My name is Mykola. I am your lecturer on this lecture. The lecture begins and ends with the words "Thank you for your visit, thanks God for our life and I love you all". If someone may seem it strange, then understand it simply and literally. This is only my positive attitude to understand, appreciate and love the life better. No more and no less. If you do not do it, if you do not determine yorself in your life, your knowledge, desires, the results will be, as in a joke. Three men got on a desert island because of the sea wreck. Two other men watched the sea, burnt the fire and tried to make any signal. One of them was praying and saying that God would save. In some time they had two boats that took each time one person. The praying man was asked to come with them twice. He only said that God would save him. One day the island has gone down under the water. The believer died and got to heaven. He saw God and asked him why? I was praying he said. The reply was: you had two boats and you did not use any. Or there is another situation. A man wanted to win a million in a lottery but he did not buy a lottery, only wanted and prayed. Getting to heaven he meets God and asks why it all happened. He received the answer that it was necessary to buy a lottery, that's it! So, the conclusion is the desire is good, but you need to do something in the direction of your wishes realization. That's why I constantly learn to understand life, feel and love it. That makes me feel sense of gratitude for all this and respect life, and myself for the results. Wish the same to you. Because these three important words – to understand, to love and to respect, all they reflect an understanding of the word "development", as experience does not disappear, but only comes! Therefore, I wish you to increase your experience, understanding, love and respect!

The Lecture, one may say, began with these words. They will be repeated again and again. As the students at the philology are trained "repetition is the mother of learning". Or taste comes during lunch))! The more you repeat, the better you know and that's the point. This happens at school with a child in mathematics lessons, reading and writing. How many times had the child to repeat to learn and understand!? It happened the same when we first sat in a car or at a bicycle. How many times did you have practice again and again in reading, writing, washing, cooking, child eating and many many other examples!? There are a lot of examples in different and various spheres of human activity. Speak any language and things will remain the same!

Determining the purpose of the lecture and audience expectations

So, our first communication in congratulations smoothly came to the next question to determine goals of the lecture and the audience's expectations. So what is the purpose of the lecture? I will repeat again its name "Human self-development. Basics". Let's answer a riddle on the basis of these words. I know that this is not difficult, but it will be interesting for you yourselves to see and may wonder how each of you is thinking about the same questions.

The question to the audience is "How do you understand the meaning and purpose of the lecture entitled "Human Self-development. The Basics"?

Lecturer's actions. He asks the audience and raises up to 10 people from different places. They answer. For example.

- Lecture will give us answers how to self-develop...
- Lecture will tell us about the basics of self-understanding...
- Lecture will give answers to many questions that a man has...

The most important basis of the above is the desire of people to get answers. Please tell me if a child can learn to hold a spoon, if his mom does it instead of him himself!? And can you ride a bike or a car if you never did it? Can a child solve a task in mathematics without trying to understand it? There is even a story that is taught in school. It tells how a man had a lazy son. Father wanted to teach him life, but how can he do it? The best way to make him work. He told his son to earn money. Son somehow or somewhere made some money. Father took it and threw it into the fireplace. There was no reaction from the son, he was only surprised and asked why he did so. The answer was simple – it was not your money, and you did not earn it. Go and earn it again. This time son worked a lot to earn a little money. When his father threw the money again into the fireplace this time, son ran to take it out with bare hands, begging not to do anymore. He earned it by his hands. Father agreed that it was his money and he appreciated it because his son earned it by himself.

Therefore, it is impossible to live without feeling this life, and just to feel it you need to work a lot, and there is even more all-around! That's why the purpose of the lecture is not to give you answers that you do not need and which you do not appreciate. The purpose is to provide components of the task and an opportunity for conscious choice of your future lifestyle. The answers can often be an easy task, but frankly speaking actually while reading the Bible you find answers not at once and each time you find new. And we or you read the same words! The question is constantly the same, wants is that a man wants!? In fact, all or most of the answers are all around us, on us and in us. But we do not so much need them if we do not know them. Therefore, the question on the first place is whether a person really wants to understand and feel that life better and more. This is the question of choice of your direction in life. You don't have to choose, but anyway you are moving that way. Life on earth, or anywhere else is not a playground, as we have conditions for creating these games.

Who's finding it difficult to understand? Let's check it out what you've understood.

- I understood that a man does not need all answers ...
- I realized that a man needs to ask himself what he really needs...
- I realized that the problem is in choosing to learn and understand, or simply play the game ...

Life is a game. You know these words. You can often hear them in films. But what do we do when teaching a child? Do we play with him or teach him live? The answer will be different. Most people will say they teach. But confess yourselves that in moments when you try to protect your child out of troubles, you hide him from the opportunity to learn how to deal with these problems more than helping him learn. And he will have to learn solve problems in future anyway. You just try to hide yourselves hiding your child. And what we do at work or in your own business? Do we just try to escape from problems? As far as I know, working in this sphere most of my life time from school, we learn and solve the problems, whatever they were, and how hard we can feel. That is why it is so difficult sometimes at work and accept our job at all! This question is for everyone and there is only you who knows the answers.

That question remains open. What makes a man caring for a child and in business? He develops and stores, or just simply enjoys without being responsible for anything, without making goals for himself, a child, or business?

The question with the answer is inside us.

Lecturer asks a few from the audience, what makes a person caring about the child and developing business?

- A man teaches a child and develops business ...
- A man cares and protects...
- A person wants to get more in business and raise a child ...

Actually this is the uncertainty of a man if he wants just to raise a child, or he wants him have some qualities and skills!? Man doubts, does not understand and transfer it all to his child since childhood. The same is happening in business and work. I don't mean all people live the same way, no, people do learn to set goals and achieve them. But is it the same achieve business goals to earn a lot of money and develop your personality and all details of human life in understanding all these details of life and all the goals?! It must be that way, but why am I telling you all this right now in this lecture? it says only that all is not so simple.

Let's summarize what is the purpose of the lecture again?
The lecturer can ask up to 10 people from audience.

The lecture is intended to show theoretical conditions of the task of human life with the practical aspects. They lie in the fact that the lecturer asks a few people in the audience what they understood from spoken moments and it determines the level of understanding of previously said. And the main purpose of the issue to show a picture of life in understanding the known components, and ask a man what he wants - learn and understand or play games, and live, not having begun to live!? Therefore, even asking, I can just tell the audience my thoughts openly. The basic message of the lecture and life is learning to live together, or play and run away, spending your life in vain and in waiting of unknown, or getting into adventures of your fantasies.

Physical and psychological preparedness. Gymnastics.

If we all are ready for the main part, let's start so to speak with gymnastics and self-programming. Everyone has heard the main objectives and the basic purpose of the lecture. If someone is somehow not interested, not satisfied or has other reasons, then feel free to safely leave the lecture and continue your life outside. Time here will waste your life, or will not satisfy your expectations. It's your opinion and decision. It may be different, however I will always be glad to see you again))! Those who consciously stay here need to forget everything and all your questions during this time. Asking the audience. You are here? Can you hear me and are willing to hear?

Audience response may be different. The basic answer is - yes.

But you want not only to hear, I want you not only could hear, but also perceive and feel. Let's set up our feelings. First, let's start with breathing and physical movements. I understand that this is best done with a small audience, but tell me what's the difference? I and mainly all you are interested in the result of the sum of your activity of the feeling and thinking. Isn't it? Therefore, get up from your seats and shake the hands with your shoulders up and down. Come on, shake a little and stir with your fingers, because they may atrophy if you do live on the same way. Everything lives for and with the help of the movement, and sure for need to live. Repeat it and understand all your being. It's better to pressure from the legs. But it is inconvenient here for you. So just shake your legs still. One and the other, one and the other. Then turn the toes of your leg clockwise and counterclockwise in turn one and the other. One two Three. All this looks good, but in fact you forgot to yourself and me clarify that results will be better in a combination of the body key components – breathing and body movement. You see and it seems that we all know. The process is the learning to understand and feel your own body. Tomorrow doesn't matter, we are here and do it now. Feel the body, feel your breath. Breathe only with your nose and do not overwork you body breathing. Breathe calmly and shake your legs again, then socks and toes clockwise and counterclockwise. Turn around the bones of hands clockwise and counter-clockwise, right, left, from yourself and to yourself. Focus on your breathing. Breath is important as the basis of your life. If you want not only to hear beautiful and wise things then do it and try to learn something practically, it's better than just reading or watching. Once again shake the shoulders as you exhale. Do it a few times until you feel the coming of fresh air into the lungs and breath of this fresh air in your nose. Then raise your hands up and drop down quietly. Inhale air deeply and necessarily belly. In general, you need to breathe with a nose only, necessarily belly. Do it necessarily belly and remember it. First, the stomach is filling from the bottom up and then gets rid of the air.

It was psychophysical training. That we will help us have more time for better results in sensations, perception and thoughts. This is the basic technical and tactical part of the work of man.

Now the question. Do you want to understand and know, or just listen? I am asking everbody and please answer me at least someone...

Audience answers with a few people.

Whatever is your choice now. More important is understanding the value of your choice until the end of the lecture. We are all adults and we know that our decisions have consequences. We should not hide from ourselves and not identify it consciously. Therefore, I feel responsibility for each of you separately and in general too. The lecture's goals are known and you know where it leads too. We need just to get there if we all understand further content and want to rethink it, check to explore. I will repeat these points constantly that you could better adopt them by your consciousness. This is public information of the objectives of such actions.

2- The main part of the lecture

What is the meaning of the word development?

We moved on to the main part of the lecture. Let's start with a simple question to the audience, "What does the word development" mean in your opinion?" We need a few answers from the audience, and ten short phrases of understanding of this word. Simple attitude, opinion or meaning.

You can hear different answers.

"It means to increase"
"It also means improving"
"It means something to develop and improve"

Answers can be different and it is important to see that the meaning of the word "development" as a process of qualitative and quantitative increase is the same in the general sense. The main requirement for shared understanding is a common understanding of the meanings of words. The word "development" means to develop something, isn't it? Asking you I will add more. This is a very important word and all of us should have a common understanding. The semantics of understanding. To develop, that is, to expand, to change for the better quality. To develop money means to increase its quantity. Everything has its meaning and purpose, depending on the scope of use. Is this important!? It is and very much. Therefore, this word has an entire sub-theme.

What can we get from our physical activity? I have already said the purpose – to feel and think. Thus, physical activity releases of excess thinking, to improve feeling and thinking. We just improve, develop feelings and thinking. We also must learn to do it and find time for this. To learn how to develop feeling and thinking to improve the sensation of your body, life around, your own thinking and, accordingly, the final perception. We will develop a better sense of life, its understanding, we will appreciate and respect it more. We're just going to enjoy and love it and everything more. Everyone needs to learn how to do it, first to study, try and create your own experience of creation of life. Another format of thinking – from survival to development and the creation, not the same.

Smile))! You deserve it. Tell me if you do agree with the above? We move, feel, understand, and again feel and understand. Thus we improve our understanding of the feeling and thinking experience and that as a result gives a sense of purpose, but it is not only a sense of purpose, it is the accumulation of experience and feelings of love as the sum of experiences and understanding with the price of respect. We just feel – know – appreciate and love.

Picture. Development pyramid

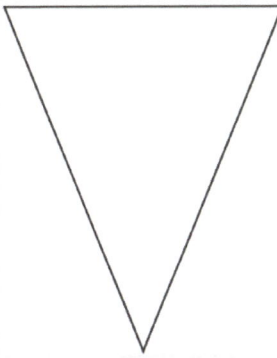

The picture shows a common increase in the level of knowledge and practical skills, that is experience. The inverted pyramid with a narrow top down, shows the evolution from smallest to largest. It is not quite as easy as it is drawn, but this will be said about, so let's go on as planned.

What is the purpose of any lecture?

In this topic, we shall only define certain facts already known to us and see how much they are already known as well. But most importantly, we shall describe a common understanding of terms and notions that we use for a better shared understanding, if we need to understand the same. After being determined to go together, we go one way at a time when we are going together.

Therefore, what is your opinion about the purpose of the lecture in general?

"The lecturer tells polls and students"

"At the seminar, we get knowledge"

The answers will be different. Each may be right in what he knows. Therefore, we should chose a common understanding. A seminar has a purpose to inform and chat. A lecture mostly report. It's allowed to respond. That is, depending on the audience and purpose of the lecture, it can be as a discussion, more by the lecturer. Lecturer gives the information that is the theory. This lecture does not differ especially. And it's not quite true. I set a goal to not only tell, but also to ensure general understanding, and partially to implement practical aspects from the listeners' side. A listener mostly listens. Do you only want to listen to and accept, or would like to join, feel and understand yourself too?! You could not answer the question before the lecture, perhaps, but I think now you have a question to investigate and understand that you hear yourself, or just to listen and forget it!

Each lecture or seminar provides theoretical knowledge that will amaze a person and he can remember it for a long time and even use in his everyday life. The more it happens the more interesting it becomes and most importantly the more meaningful the life is. After all, when the person has more questions and challenges it brings more experience, respect and love.

So, seminars are a collective means of educating people, better say information transfer. They won't ever become more effective than individual or group classes because there is individual work, or relatively close to the individual personality traits. Work with someone individually brings the best results for all involved. Everyone has questions of his own, needs, thinking and attitude. Therefore it's quite difficult to respond to any requests at public seminars and lectures.

A good example is with school. When there is a lot of children, it is difficult to look after them. This is natural and understandable. Here it is necessary to rely on the ability of a person, his level of experience and development as well. But people pay little attention at the development. What understanding can you have in what you take little interest and are not engaged almost at all. Who can be named as a scholar of life, a man who constantly and systematically improves the system experience of his own life and life around? If you think in general, then perhaps we all people do it every day. But then ask yourself how it is systematically towards you, as a human personally! That is details that we didn't not just learn and understand for the hundredth time, more or less. This should be details literally to every detail of you and your life. If that were like that, there would not be this lecture and to be honest, I personally would be more happy to study it with someone and not be move independently, and with fear before other people. Imagine now that you had or you have developed additional features, some supernatural powers. This would be your curse against people to whom it's hard to understand and realize. You would be lonely, or somebody would use you. Just as you would not quite understand what to do about this and would do what you can. You can heal the you will heal, you can be psychics you will. But the question of what it is and how to treat your development as well as a question of your development would not be closed! It would stand sharper.

In this case, I like movies and TV shows about vampires. Especially Vampire Diaries. A good series about love, relationships and eternity. That's a big seminar series so much that you can be tired of watching! It's true, but life won't ever bother us, will it))?! Life goals and development results also depend on it. Each lecture, movie, our personal life stories are seminars and lectures as well where we even participate. This is more interesting. It's much more interesting to feel, empathize, understand, or rack your brains to understand. Then to understand, respect and love, isn't it)?! Yes, of course. Sometime or often our indifference to understand the importance of feeling and understanding leads us to extremes and therefore we make stupid and lose important to us. We suffer again, live and learn to understand, or just get disappointed and crumple up. It is always easier to do.

To participate by your own feelings, to learn understand, to become stronger, to have more experience, to respect more your own experience and all around, to love yourself, everyone and everything around is more important for dry and indifferent contemplation, temporary interest, loss of life meaning, frustration, misunderstanding and fear, isn't? Think about yourself and admit it in your soul. It influences whether you want to understand something and live?

Further is more interesting))).

How paints an artist a picture?

I am asking the audience to tell briefly, literally two or three sentences about stages of drawing, for example landscape?

People raise their hands and tell their own experience. Many of them can be artists. They will point to the drawing stages. Someone will express thoughts. All matters. This is a strange and important experience. Others who can not draw will get this experience as picture's understanding, as these processes occur in someone else's sphere of activity. To hear at lecture systematic structure and highlight the main elements of the gradual formation of vision and paintings' reproduction. The word "system" in this topic plays an important and crucial role. This understanding has been interpreted by other examples. Now we can use this word for a complex understanding of the drawing processes, thinking, vision and feeling. Every activity has its own sequence of execution, has a lot of elements and components that you need to learn to use to create a beautiful picture. For example, you need to know how to use a pen or pencil, too, for drawing. Then you have to learn and choose instruments to draw. You can use paper for the initial drawings, for better artistic skills an artist chooses canvas. Then there are different kinds of brushes and a lot, a lot of different things that you might need, or at least they are important for the artist. Any activity, even the normal dressing especially drawing acquires more and tools and experience with time in the use and creation of a good kind of dress and beautiful paintings on canvas.

For example, look at the following two pictures.

Picture.

I call these pictures simple vision of stages of drawing playback. They are a bit simple and not deep, respectively. Professional artists can better evaluate the image data in this context. This is his sphere of creation and thinking. It shows what elements are necessary to depict and modify for better perception. First you can not understand a picture, because it does not show the final shapes. As well as life is formed in the imagination gradually with time and troublesome work. The artist paints a picture step by step and gradually over time, giving it better visibility and content.

Let us note important points. Everything that surrounds us accommodates information. Over time, we learn to read and understand it, explain and use. Man is constantly creating new knowledge. He has many activities and becomes more professional preferably in one sphere. And he really does. Man gets and creates a system of understanding things. The usual choice of clothing turns into a partition of all important components for which you need to buy and wear. An artist becomes a painter as well with time. He gradually gains experience. To become a better artist, he should draw more and learn new things in this field of art. The more he draws the better begins to see the world from the other side, just a little different. An accountant gets such vision that helps to become more precise in his thinking, a farmer who works with animals and plants and study their behavior gets the same. The driver watches the world through car's window in motion and learns to be careful and have a better response. The artist, in turn, has its own vision and even the rhythm of life. If you recall the yogis and yoga, the feeling of the body and state of mind especially after school change your impression and perception of life. But in this case, as with students and children in general, constant work and study, and use have a significant difference. Mother teaches and preserves her child. The same while practicing yoga for a better sense of body and soul a person feels and learns, but if he does not create anything, does not teach and develop skills, to create skills and experience becomes difficult. As well as to learn to draw, if you don't create your own pictures and don't improve them, then the skills and knowledge do not develop and grow qualitatively and quantitatively that form the invaluable experience of improving one element. And can you draw a picture with one element? If you learnt to draw flowers, how are you going to draw the sky or people? If you take another contrasting example, then without a pencil or brush, as well as without canvas, there won't be any picture then. Each element that contributes to the drawing to get a good picture, has its value in time and the work plan.

Even the mood of the artist may affect his art. While recalling the general attitude of doing the job for which you are paid, you can remember that a person feels the need and commitment to someone else, as well as responsibility for the result. He often makes himself to work and get the desired results. He may not always like it. Entrepreneurs have a different attitude. They provide services and sell goods. A store owner can open and close his shop at any time. He does not owe anything to anybody. But when new shops are beginning to appear, natural competition starts to appear and the owner of a shop starts to respect more his clients, to take care of the quality and range of goods, and he voluntarily becomes responsible for his decisions. The artist as well as any person who has his own sphere of activity is often difficult to live without such responsibilities. Then even the weather can spoil the mood and desire to paint and create. Only with time and the great work he experiences ability to see pictures of reality, in his own head before his eyes, to reproduce these pictures and put the soul in his masterpieces. When he can show people and motivate with his art. When he describes in the art not just an image, but attitude, feeling of soul and mind, emphasizing technical expertise drawing.

The artist begins to see his own stages of formation and development through drawing. Someone does through yoga, book writing, business, just living and other activities. There are many variants, but we forget to remember one important and essential thing. The artist uses tools to shape the experience, to reflect on the canvas of life and his attitude and vision of its colors, beauty and cruelty. The artist creates not just a picture. He forms his personality through the picture, and when he begins to forget about it, that's when his pictures and desires start to remind him about that with the lack of meaning in his work, with mood changes and dissatisfaction. After all, a person uses tools to learn how to use them and to create a product, as a parallel cloning of himself. He often forgets that at work and the work build a content of his soul and its capabilities. Painting and other tools are just tools. The artist draws a picture, and not vice versa.

Painting system is a system of forming the personality of the artist and his content. To paint a picture you need a tool, desire, ability, time and purpose...

What needs for the formation of a man? What is it from? Such rhetorical questions at this stage. They will be repeated and the key word in this topic is the word "system", as the sum of interrelated parts that you need to know and learn to use them to create your picture of life.

Let's check out if we understand the said above well! I am putting the question to the audience how paints an artist a picture? Share a few words that come to your mind and do not even think about it, just say It. You will see how you respond. You'll be creating your own thinking in the move, which eventually becomes more meaningful and simply better!

Question: how paints an artist a picture?

"The artist imagines and gradually reproduces"
"The artist draws and begins with the background"
"The artist gradually reproduces its own vision and experience on the canvas, along with desire and mood"

Good answers. If to form understanding with words, it will be the beginning of the formation of your vision's picture, your desires, dreams, the formation of experience, knowledge... These words and your statement are an art to hide your identity and its formation through picture's words and their meanings. Everyone is an artist and has a lot of tools to create a better person of yourself with the best opportunities and doesn't cease to improve the quantity and quality of his craftsmanship. That's beautiful and it's worth to appreciate, to develop and create a whole system of experience, knowledge, understanding and tools to develop a better picture of human life – the man. It looks selfish, but it is not. These words only emphasize the importance of understanding to reckon with the fact what is a man, what he has and what he can do in details. This is the great goal of art in any area of life that you need to understand, appreciate and love. It will come by itself, because experience creates knowledge, understanding, feeling that improve constantly layers, contents, meaning of understanding, taking away unnecessary things. It gives pleasure and thus the feeling of love and respect...

Therefore, I beg you to summarize what you have understood for yourself in this topic and I was trying to say and express! Which is or what main points, concepts, in your opinion, was I laying in this topic?

Ask to yourselves first. This will be the practical point in the moment of your development. You didn't just listen but you remembered something, took into account, or just took an interest in, and it'd be better if you asked yourselves. Pay a special attention to these items and perhaps better even write down. And now answer me and tell me your thoughts on this question.

Which or what the main points, concepts, in your opinion, was I laying in this topic?

Answers can and will be different, the main thing is to notice whether everything the lecturer says in general coincides with the understanding of the audience. If someone does not really match, then no big deal. They can read a book, come again to the lecture, register for a seminar, group or individual lessons, or time will come when a man finally begins to understand the very basics of life. He will come then, or will ask about it himself. He will find his way and will make his choice in any case. This will be said later more. All is just being revealed, we have a lot of time and opportunity to explore new concepts. Important is the attitude – to explore, to take an interest and to study than ... to treat the consequences.

Development in business

Getting to a new topic, we again start with ourselves and practical aspects of self-development. Otherwise, what are we doing here, why to read or listen to it all))!? Who cares of it all?!

So I've got a question to you, tell me briefly what means development in business?
"Business mostly develops product's range"
"Business also develops the image, attitude toward yourself, to product and service"
"Business improves market conditions and develops quality of products and services"

The answers will be different as usual and they are all important. What you or I should even record. The answer is important for every human being as a means to express oneself and to form one's product understanding of things. This will be the beginning of a conversation about this good and important part of human life.

All you said expresses your understanding, attitude, desire and disappointment. You put into your words not only something surface that you say, but what is in your soul. And it will be more important to think about your own words, what they mean and what you put in them. Think about the question and your own opinion. You have enough life time, and we all have it too. Think and highlight key points, theses or main points in understanding. Then take a look at them from aside. Do not be afraid, no one but you will see them)).

Let's take a look at the practical level, that is, without relying on my experience, we shall form shared experience. Let's start by selecting the important components of the topic. Development in business includes business and development. We shall start with the basics of understanding the business and its creation, to look at it from aside so to speak, and accept those important details from aside. We shall talk about the goal of the business, its creation, its management and of course we shall make conclusions, or relations to a man himself.

The first question will start immediately. What is a business? What is the development of a business?

Business means a human self-activity when he produces, buys or sells something, doesn't he?! You can, for example, go into the forest and gather up mushrooms for sale. You can grow potatoes or other vegetables for sale. You can buy products cheaper and sell them more expensive, searching a buyer. This is more simple and reliable proven for centuries scheme, which is used by most businesses. There is a variety of business and it has a basic understanding of its creation - supply and demand. If products or services are required with public, they will stay as long as they are in demand or don't make losses.

Thus, at present, business is also called projects. This in my opinion is even more correct, because it helps a person to understand better what to focus on. You can name with business any commercial activity. In fact, it's not so important in this context. Of course, everything has a meaning, but we do not develop the terminology, so it is more important to make thought's expression and its understanding.

Business as a project is of great importance in understanding better planning. This is the project that requires better planning in the 21st century within sufficiently high level of competition. It merely adds to the importance of understanding to calculate losses and possible gains. There are no guarantees except your experience or a professional in this field. Though the professional can afford not to understand that kind of business, but just be good to organize, systemize, and actually sell you as an activity with an established system of work. For it is a different thing to plan and as well start your business, another thing is to manage it all the time. Relations between people are not that simple too. Not enough just to get acquainted and think that every person may be suitable for long-term relationships. Sometimes your love may not be enough, because if you don't have your interest and desire, there is no desire and understanding to you, tell me what shall we have from it?! Whatever you'd have but income and expenses are considered in business. If you do your business badly and make losses, then your balance can easy say how much time you have for work. The same is to work and lose it. You'll stay without a job until you can or lose your money to zero.

So, you cannot work and know what you can do without planning and money counting. When we come to the checkout, we can make any dreams of expensive things or a large number of products... We cannot physically give more than we have, and what is the point in doing impossible!? We can watch such things on TV or in cartoons, or dream. By the way, looking at the sky, you can be an artist and you do not need the canvas and even paint. It takes some time, in fact a lot of time from 2-4 hours in the first few days until you see those pictures that will charm you. You will draw with your imagination and see them, and it would be so exciting that you will not care of anything else then. Very good exercise, but it's so hard to do it often...

So, business projects are considered to count better if you want to know how much you need to spend funds on opening the project and its temporary activity. I personally investigated these issues in practice, working in business since 9th grade. I tried a lot of options and got different experience. In the university I often read stories about famous people and wondered how they opened their business and how it was. The question is always in the unknowns ide. But when you have questions, it is the most important part. If you have questions in life to something and you want to find an answer, you need only time and direct or relative activity. Experience comes with time and understanding of the difference what is a work, a business and a hobby they also come through desire and aspiration to understand what it is and what it all means. Only with time I realized that I can start almost any business. Important is the desire to work on it, to develop and to know its value in expenses and revenues. Each business needs various investments and has different results over time. But having tried to understand how to do business, to work at job, as a hired man, and to create your own, it becomes clear the fact that any business projects simply need to count and plan. You can develop any project, regardless of the competition. There is a classic of business stability and universal laws.

Each project aims to provide services, to sale or purchase products. All this activity needs effort, time and money. The most important question in this topic is the ability to count. Therefore we can put the question of what is business back again and answer this is a set of tools with services and products to meet the buyer's needs. That is, each project has a goal to satisfy a person's and others' needs. A man shows himself through the products and develops himself through the ability to use it, create, sell and develop. It is worth remembering that everyone faces the problem of self-organization lack. Just take a look around to other people who work in other areas, and maybe you buy something from them and often wonder yourself how people can be so inconsiderate, confused, scattered, rude and impolite. But if you look at yourself from the side of your customers and people around with whom you are dealing, they also may not like everything. That's the way we all live in this world and what do we do in business or at work? What are we doing there? Do we sell, buy or produce? Business sells, buys and produces, and a man often prevents from doing business well feeling like a stranger and cannot find himself there. Not everyone is happy with everything, not everything fits. Work disciplines and develops our skills to live our lives and create it more or less independently, and the man is sitting at work and complaining that he never has enough or something doesn't fit! Yeah, something really doesn't fit and will not always do, but just to make us move and start doing something and to create ourselves satisfied. Maybe we should change our job, make us organized, self-determined, develop skills and just enjoy life and work as it is! You need it to learn something, and the problem is not in work. The work was created by another person and his system of works is not so clear, maybe, and has a lot of bugs and unfinished moments. It's alright. You can improve this work and working system by yourself. So you will improve yourself as a system of understanding.

Each work has tasks, money and products, which you are working with. Every business as well as your handbag's content contains something. You can not always even know what it is. If you look at somebody's computer, women handbag, order in your house, at the workplace and in your tasks, you can see how much garbage each person holds in himself and how much it leaves for work, but the difference between business and work on the yourself is in fact that nobody pays you for work with yourself. The person received everything from life from his childhood and living his life can not calculate what he received from life for life, and what he learned to use!? This is a rhetorical question and is very important for everyone. The business purpose contains of the ability to simplify the work and its audit. To know what business owns and not to get confused we must learn to count and do it permanently. This is work with information and I haven't really seen well-functioning system of work so that people were not overloaded by the amount of information. That's why people often search a new job where there is less need to record their activities. It's tiring and draining. This is and I agree with that, that's why I've been working for over 10 years to create an alternative audit. I found out later that it's not necessary to do a finished product, because the scheme is more important. The scheme is and will always be universally simple, especially when the aim is to audit with a minimum amount of information entered, and time spent and to get the maximum information needed. The years of practical development of such a system showed that it is more than possible and even one person can use it for work, art, just to understand better his life with it, for accounting, and for understanding what he owns and what needs from life at all. Better to have your life written down than to have it in hazy clouds of your own thoughts and dreams that like air can dissipate in the next moment, and no one will ever tell you what you wanted or planned, something important, or just wanted to do right. In the same way, but more difficult you can manage enterprises, factories, large and small business, even a whole country with all its needs through a similar scheme, which never forgets anything, doesn't make mistakes, and even cause people to develop themselves. This is similar to the life around, but in writing. This scheme has been running for more than 7 years in my own needs and other enterprises, but a part of scheme.

The purpose of the question gives unambiguous results and everything is constantly being checked on me and others. Business gets better with a man who develops his personality and life through this business or work that he as a person often does not appreciate and not developing his work in his area, does not develop himself in the first place. The purpose of business to provide the best services doesn't prove its value in this case, because a man has not learned to count his things, to know what he is worth his life, what he wants and therefore he does not know, fears, doubts and behaves to just spoil his results. Therefore, the purpose of business is primarily to learn to count all details and improve their interaction with the attitude in the positive direction. Something can be done if you wish to do it. And when you just don't like your job, you do not love all the problems you have and which you, as a human being, create daily, it all says only that you are annoying, but not interested and do not open the door your own experience. You just do not attach importance that you gain experience every day, maybe not much, but you need it to know better what and why you are doing in your work and in your life. Only this experience will give you the opportunity to understand what you are and what you want. And it helps you feel ease of understanding, confidence, respect to experience and yourself, which of course will improve health, ease of the mood, attitude, and will increase the feeling of love and enjoyment of your life. Life will be filled with every drop of your experience and your small or large knowledge, works, thoughts and actions. After all, they form you from inside. If you do not know what you want, it's not scary and you should consider if there is no purpose, you can simply learn and enjoy what we have. Time and work will show up your knowledge, what you learned and created. Do not reduce the importance of the fact that learning to dress yourself is also important, do make-up, or be able to install software in the PC. You are what you know and know how to do it. Therefore it's worth to count what you have and respect your likes and dislikes. When doing something you do not like, then over time you can at least understand that you really don't like it and open up other possibilities. Follows them more confidently!

Goals in business, as in personal life, are based on the ability to assume what – the goals –comprise, based on and whether they ever exist.

I would like to add briefly about starting a business. It's always difficult to do something for the first time. To search for a new job, to make a task at your work, a client's order, to use a phone, or even to use conventional heater wisely, so to speak. However, when you try to do it second time again, you start to remind your experience and start your practical work to memorize the sequence of actions. New actions without experience and even with experience do not imply the absence of errors. Best experience only helps to realize they can be and you must learn to work and solve them. Moreover, when you do not have that invaluable experience, it is always difficult to say and do what you do not know and do not understand and have no particular desire to do it. For example, a teacher asks a student if he liked the subject, such as a foreign language. When the student knows this subject badly and doubts his knowledge the answer will be that he does not understand it, even better he does not like, and can be more frankly that he has not studied it. In fact, every person can be the same, if he hasn't understood and has little experience. He just does not know and is not confident. The man will never say more than he knows, so there is nothing to be surprised about. It is and only moments when he starts to count what he knows make unknown become less. So, if you do not count at the checkout you don't know what to expect and how much money to spend. And if you don't clean your room, or anything you have, your understanding and knowledge won't ever become more simple to know what you have and why. Therefore, the actual theme of the business is the best way to describe life problems of a man, his business and his attitude, and indicates development of human life and the life in which the person is.

To create a business just like to win a girl or open an orgasm can be easily and can be just as difficult, depending on desires and aspirations to understand something, to learn something, to love and to feel, to calculate and to evaluate...

What develops business and what is a development in business? If we have already talked about the ability to count and its importance, you should immediately ask what includes or is directed to that development in business?! You can develop the range and quality of products, equally important, if not the most important thing is to remember about the image and respect, which are formed over years and depend on the quality of services provided, courtesy and relationship to the customer and cooperation, to problem situations. If it was important to create a business, its support and development depends on the schemes of work and all components of the system. Relations in the collective and personal life of employees especially the director are reflected in the confidence of business and its development. Employees will destroy all created without a leader. You can't do everything yourself without the workers. No customers is no profit. Without a positive customers' response there will not be sustainable profits. Without satisfied employees there will not be the quality of services and the quantity of results. Without experience in relation and task managing there will not be responsibility.

Picture. Selection.

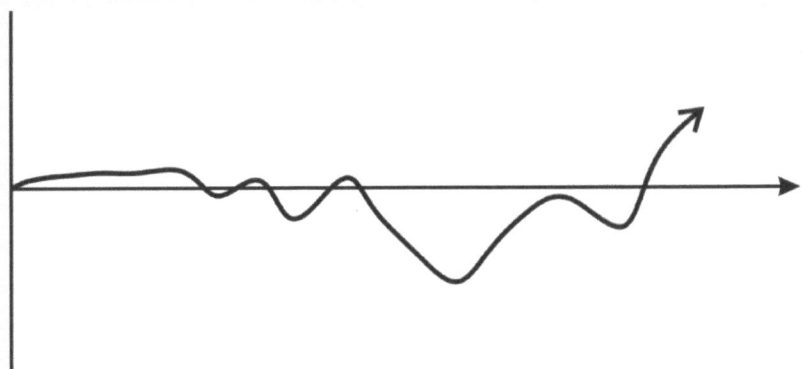

The picture shows a curve that reflects positive and negative results. This curve reflects understanding, choice, attitude and of course results of our knowledge and skills to count what we have and what we need. The curve can always be directed for better and for worse, and probably everybody can agree that it turns faster and easier for worst. If it were so easy for better, but in the better direction you need to learn to understand clothing brands, cars, bikes, cosmetics and so on. Business, as work and planning, also teaches us to respect and count, to understand how much we need it, what we lose and gain, it teaches us to be more responsible and confident. How else, when you have done so many mistakes to learn how to count))! But it should have been and should be. How should a child learn to hold a spoon and not being dirty if he's even never held the spoon!? And making dirty shows mothers experience, as the first thing that children make. They don't know how to hold a spoon. Try to be perfect in creation of what you do not know how to do, or you did it seldom to be so sure!

Question to the audience. What are the main important and significant details you can select from the above?
"You must learn to plan your business "
"Business is developing providing products»
"Business creates a man in business"

Other answers will be different and they are important, too, to see what a man took for himself and at what stage he is. Everyone will understand something of his own at his time, and so it should be.

Next question. What connection is between people and business?
"Man creates business"
"Man develops business and himself"
"Man must learn to count money and his own experience"

The answers will be different for each. It is important to note what has not been said. It's worth just to summarize what is important in business. What is the most important thing in business? The most will say a profit. Then I'll put a new question, what will you get with the profit? You will have new and bright and sometimes perverted desires, won't you? I bet you will and this is a natural way to discover your personality and development. Personality depends on external factors. Profit is only one factor and it is important to understand. What makes this profit? The quality and quantity of products and services, as final indicators of interaction between the company and the client. We must learn to develop profit, and misunderstanding of normal developmental processes will stop the business scheme for a while, or until complete or partial destruction. Therefore, when a person stops at answer and need to make a profit, he forgets that it is only one element of his life including business and work. Definitely you need to have the counting experience and to count once again... Business is as complex and self-sufficient element, as the man himself. If a person looks in the mirror, he will see him reflected there. The same reflecting can be seen through man's business and work. It should always be remembered that a person is constantly improving and lives, what will be discussed later about.

Human development and its components.

Probably the most difficult topic of this lecture. Human development and its components. We have researched and talked about the understanding of development as a sign of the overall increase in qualitative and quantitative changes. We've spoken and understood that everything has its purpose and its goal. We are well aware that the goal is based on the need. If you do not like for example milk or alcoholic beverages, they may not even exist for you. And anything that is not required for use will not ever be created. We are going by train, where each next car pushes the previous one, and as each brick is laid down after previous one to make a wall. This way the artist draws his picture and every day we make a daily variety of actions, dress, cook, work, and do not think about how it happens. It's simple and understandable for us, and therefore we do not see it.

And in business we emphasized the meaning and the importance of understanding the system components that interact and create a certain sequence. Brick after brick makes a house and if the house will have a hole that should not be there, so it was badly planned and done, wasn't it? Therefore, it's worth not only to enjoy the process of life, but learn to look deeper and to understand how everything works to build your pyramid of experience from childhood

Picture. Experience's pyramid

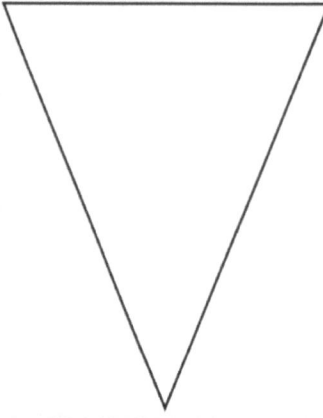

Look at the pyramid from the bottom up from the lower part to the greater. The child grows and grows his experience, to put it briefly. Gradually, over the years, people get richer experience. What has a person from birth? Look around and at yourself. Think about what you actually increase in your lives from birth and what is constantly referred to in various wise books, and what you do remember every time about, especially at work, or in business?! Development in business does not surprise a person. He understands that new work is a new experience, and so the person gathers experience drop by drop all his life, and there arises a question, whether he gets tired of knowledge and the amount of information and gets confused in understanding why it is so much and what is all this for? With an increase in information, or even means people do not always know what to do with them. Therefore, we will not afford to wrestle with and continue our research. Actually it is better to call that you did sit passively perceiving and indifferently wasting your time to play without any need to understand what it's all about.

Throw away your experience. How to do it? Imagine that you are not using your experience and knowledge. You are getting to new knowledge and are building your own. You do not need extra thoughts except the task to understand what you can see, hear, read and perceive just now. Use only when necessary your efforts to remember and to compare. Set aside, let's get together plunge into the formation and building of the house from bricks' task. I give these elements to find solutions, or do you think you came to hear answers, you do not need? In fact, you will not hear, even if they are told, because you simply will not perceive them, that's why as much as you need to create a new experience together with me for a better understanding for all of us and individually for each one?! Throw away your thoughts and knowledge, and let's unravel the puzzle you need, let's find out what you really need...

None becomes indifferent to the question of sensations of imposing opinions, or someone else's desire to deceive you. So if you really need to form your own opinion and see the bricks that are to form new and larger in scale, let's consider carefully the conditions of the task or questions that are given. Otherwise, you will deceive your selves in your lack of understanding. You concentrate your attention at work on a task, don't you?!

When a child is born. What does he know?! If he is born in the body, and the body has given experience in its own structure, and in an environment that produces the man, so, it becomes possible to represent the overall picture of human needs. A man and the ability to think originally form our needs and requirements for behavior in our life. When an animal's baby is born, it almost immediately gets up onto its feet and begins to walk. It does not understand much, but the volume of thinking also differs from human. You can compare a calculator, a mobile smart phone and a computer. They differ from each other and that's no surprise. If a person needs only to call, then why are other functions, if you are not using them! In such a case, a person buys a simple phone for calls. When he developed the capabilities and needs to use large amounts of information, then he buys something modern, which can take advantage of additional features to make photo, video, or even something to print and work.

We will not just be much in a hurry and overload thinking with thoughts about anything, but we'll summarize what was said. Man is born with minimal knowledge and needs, he gradually develops and learns to crawl, walk, talk, eat, dress, read, write and speak. So we should take a look again at the picture of the inverted pyramid and understand that from less side a man develops himself and grows up his experience to the larger side. But we are meaning thinking more! Yes, because the human body is used as a means to obtain information and new sensations. It's more like a car that you buy for learning to drive. The fear of death and the loss of money spent on it is pushing a man to drive a car. Maybe not, but... Something always causes a person to fear and worry about. But the man knows, or at least learns to understand what is that "something"!? This is what we'll talk later.

Let's look at a picture of life, or the environment where a person comes. We will just turn around the pyramid, and then combine them even.

Picture. Pyramid in Pyramid

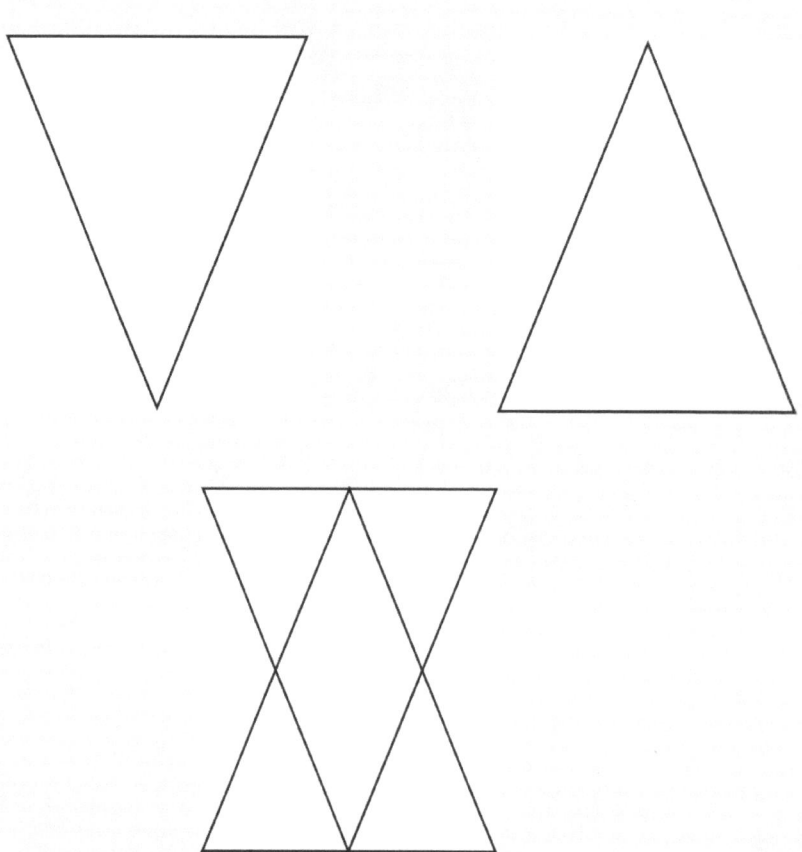

Pyramid top down shows the development of a man from birth. That is, the development of zero relatively. Next pyramid with top peak denotes an environment, in which the man himself is born. The environment is called environment because it has everything needed to create the desired item. If a person is hungry, he seeks and creates food, such as airplanes and other mechanisms and tools. Environment creates needs in a dynamic movement. Therefore, a person is born at the foot of the pyramid in the ready environment, where is down, not top of the pyramid.

Moving on to the next drawing I will comment its purpose – to unite needs. A man is born at the foot of the pyramid with ready capabilities and information to study them. Animal or plant, all are born and adapt to life in these conditions. Man is characterized by a qualitative indicator that he is capable to understand needs of the environment's root. After all, every pyramid has a middle. In general, all has the middle, as the content that is embedded therein.

Man from his birth deals with the ready environment and prepared information that he needs to take to pieces and learn. Anyway, the body and the environment push to it with the threat to human life. Everybody wants to live. The theme "Development of human life" contains three key words: development, as an increase in the opportunities, life, as a movement, actions and a man, as a tool.

The joint pyramid shows what a person is born with and how he develops in gaining experience.

A good example will be the child's birth and his education, business creation and development, the soul's experience creating in the human body. The human development capabilities at the picture of the inverted pyramid down increases. The amount of environment's information for human life decreases, but if you remember the cyclical nature and the interaction, then it will mean that a person can not get the experience, if he does not create it, doesn't develop himself. This is the most important point in understanding of the entire lecture. The word "development" means to create something in the best quality. But here lies the interaction of different circumstances. For example a child learns to walk better with time and with each step. The number of errors in a child's life gives him the best quality and development of capabilities, which will be the foundation of confidence and skills, at least in this example - to walk.

Let's look at life from a different scale, with generalized understanding.

Picture. Components of human life.

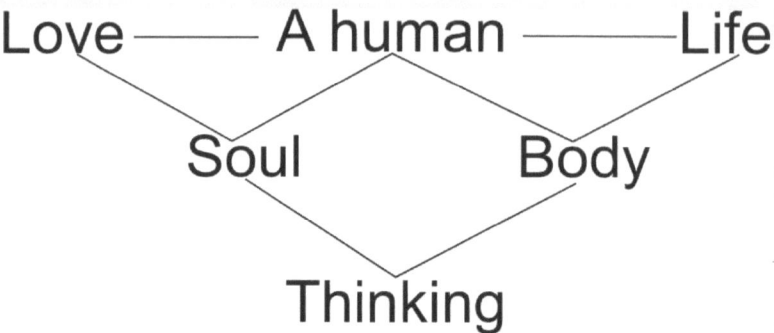

Look at the picture. Everything has its meaning. Life creates a man to improve the quality of human love as the end point of the meaning. We can say in other words. What is love? What is life? And what is a human being? If you try to use another variant, it is possible to say that a person is in the middle between the environment's possibilities and love in harmony of interaction and development. This scheme represents a link between basic concepts and how they interact. A man composes of body and soul in a general sense. And between them, in the basis of all not only a human being is the thinking as a process of generating information. Maybe it's not a quite perfect explanation, but the important thing is the content that can always be improved in depth of understanding.

The man is between a sense of love, a sense in general and life, as movement.

What are the similarities between the computer that man created and man? They have a body and have energy, which carries information and creates it. Body, energy and information are in one. Environment is an external factor in creating needs and opportunities.

Perhaps another image will help a little to supplement a certain picture of understanding.

Picture.

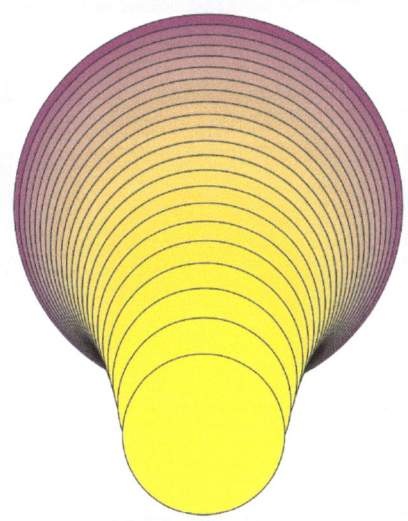

The picture shows the cyclic human development and the formation of his experience. As a brick is laid around a circle, the same with human questions, his own experience creates circles of his own formation. When a person cannot buy a brick for the next round, then it will not be laid out, and the house will remain unfinished. The human formation of experience has no difference. Put questions must be completed, otherwise next experience will be formed. Because the previous result should be the foundation for the next. And so the pattern repeats until the circle after circle will not build a wall of understanding. The following image shows the principles of questions construction and human needs.

Picture. System

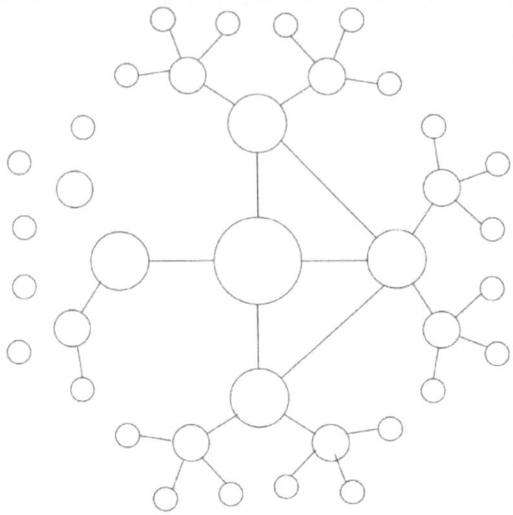

The picture shows a system of experience's formation, the system of relationships forming and interactions between components. Previous image showed the ring from aside, as if the house from the outside. This image shows a top view, shows time and even the development of human questions, needs and desires. First there is several of them, as well as needs. When a person begins to increase questions and answers they are beginning to form the following questions, desires and dreams, which may well remain dreams and have no relevance to the individual needs.

For example, a person develops experience in work, business, etc., but at the same time he forgets to take care of his own body, or he does not develop a feeling through love and relationships in family relations. It is important to note that a person can learn German language, which he does not use and will never use, respectively these skills will be gradually growing and will also be forgotten.

For example, take a piece of paper in your free time and write the word "desire" in the middle. You can write there dreams, goals, plans, questions to life, interests and anything you like. It will be more important to set a goal in the middle of the paper to determine the direction of thinking and gathering information. Your brain will collect everything that interests you and all that you can or can not require. During such actions there is no need to think about rationality of written, just write down, you need to set a goal and just write whatever you hear from your head and heart together. You will see a picture of your questions and experiences.

Then think about what you know about these questions and why you need them at all. All unnecessary links will be lost in your imagination and you will no longer think and do what makes your life meaningless and does not expand your opportunities. But in saying this I mean that you have a lot of questions, or relatively a big amount, and to separate out only one or a few for your life you should do while achieving goals.

After clarifying important questions for you, you will see what you want and can do, but can it be enough? The next round will consist already defined questions and answers that you wrote around the main question. The second round will touch every answer and it will show you the depth of your knowledge and desires. There are third and subsequent circles, and so you can see yourseves as you are aware of, what you have and what is missing.

Other questions, rather components of your life can not do without your attention. You cannot and should not forget about the body and what it needs, as well as need to understand it more, learn and listen to. Your soul feels the world through the body and interacts with the environment. If you remove the body, the soul remains as a closed person in a room with no windows and doors, through which you could contemplate and even feel the outside world. Therefore, you need to count and take into account the fact what a person has at his disposal is just necessary to feel qualitatively better results of interaction and experience's development through the world ...

Asking you as the audience I'd like to summarize the story and research, I can only ask you to briefly sum up and say, if you made a picture of understanding? The next topics will be more interesting. They will continue to go into details of our lives and that is the question of self-education.

Table of negative and positive and its value

Therefore, in the subject about the negative we will focus a little more on the issue of negative and positive in human life. Throughout lecture we frequently mentioned development, money, actions and consequences. Let's say a business is considered more as money, although it is not so, but it is the basic unit. And how can you measure a man?

Remind yourself the human life components table as well as a man in the same table, the system of human development and time periods?

How to measure a man and his life? What unit or concept should be selected as the basis?

Give yourself the answer and tell me your thoughts out loud. You may not think much and just say the first thing that comes to mind. It will be your best answer to a question that you do not know. If you know the answer, of course it's another matter. It's like to make your first thing out of paper, wood or something. Even cooking is not the matter at one time. Everyone probably understands this, especially when faces this. The first time will not always be the best the same as the next one, but with time and practice they will get better. The same with thoughts. The second thought having comprehended the first one will be better and the next one will always make a better content, will supplement something and will take it away, but will be formed in the best quality with lots of facts and practical examples.

So, we talked about the general structure of human life and a man himself. In physics you can remember that each object is made up of smaller parts and of the smallest visible particles, I apologize for not quite correct formulation. It is called a molecule, which in turn has its own structure. Let's look at the picture.

Picture. Atomic Structure

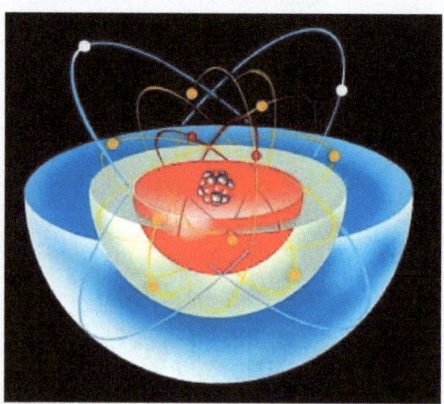

Other similar images of atom

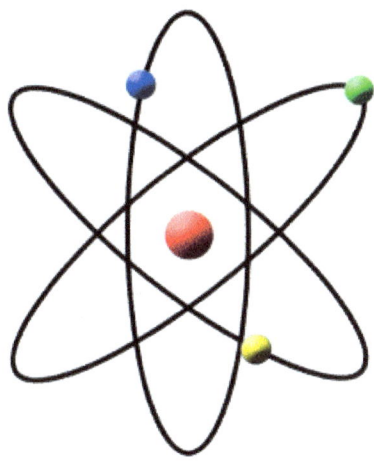

The pictures show the atomic structure that consists of a nucleus and electrons moving around like planets around the sun. In practice they are very similar. The nucleus itself has an even deeper meaning and consists of light and even smaller parts. This is how the whole world consists of, which has a different scope and can accommodate a large range of worlds, opportunities and levels.

Everything that surrounds us is composed of many parts and even worlds, as already mentioned. Now you can imagine what the man is in the sum of all those worlds and parts. Man technically managed to see a little bit of 10^{-20}, as I know. This is not exact information. The light part, which is the minimum, is significantly less. It is somehow calculated. It can certainly much better describe the world's structure. This concept is very important not only to scientists, but also to ordinary people who think that the world is incomprehensible and has no clear parameters, or think that it is ideal and stable. That all what a man sees around himself is the way he describes in his head. All these issues are relative and relative within their scope understanding and opportunities to use them and manipulate.

An opportunity to learn, the ability to get to the core issues and understand the problem gives an incredible opportunity for the development of human thinking and accordingly of him in total. Man cannot say, do and imagine more than he has in his head. If you never saw an elephant and never heard such words, then how do you know what it is? At the same time, it exists independently of your submission because others know. You may not know it, and what others know. Remind yourself of the pyramid, and you can see that you do not have necessarily to know everything. The primary human task is to understand and imagine to make a form and meaning of the object. And that's the way everything is created. The same way you plan events, run some daily tasks. First, you set a goal to understand components and their content. Then the question is to find solutions. Pretty simple, but when you have experience and only when a person does not know and does not understand becomes clear that the issue becomes complicated and confusing.

For example, it is easier and more important for a person to understand what attracts his attention, than what has less meaning in his opinion. You want or not, but working questions you need to solve, to learn to use programs, to select clothes, to speak and behave in society. However, the question of your body and soul needs sensations are put into the background, and mostly are not considered as existing. Religious books tell us about the soul more, as practical experience can help you understand your life and realize human needs. If you don't make emphasis on it and don't investigate it scientifically, then there is no need to pay great attention on this. Therefore, you can understand where your illness comes from only from doctors who certainly know a lot, but if it is necessary for the development of your body and soul is not a fact. Responsibility for the health and human life meets the man himself. After all, when you can cure yourself or your eyes at home, none of doctors will not benefit, because that does not bring money. To sum up, why do you have to get ill if you can develop body and soul!? It's quite a different attitude and direction of thinking. Compare it please to survive and create, develop! Two opposite sides that exist simultaneously.

Let's take a look at the picture.

Picture. Positive negative.

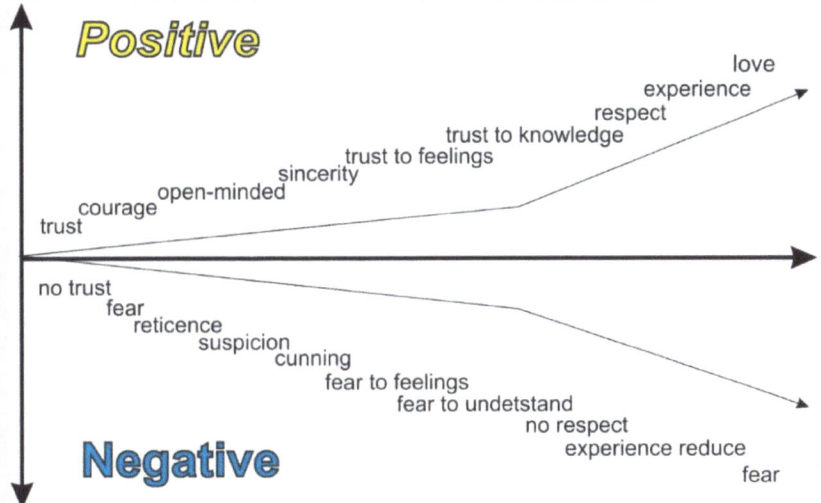

This is the first picture in the history of its creation, although is not the very first one. I had different attempts of another sort. Over time, everything can be improved when it is already there, so there is the following picture with completion.

Picture. Positive negative 2.

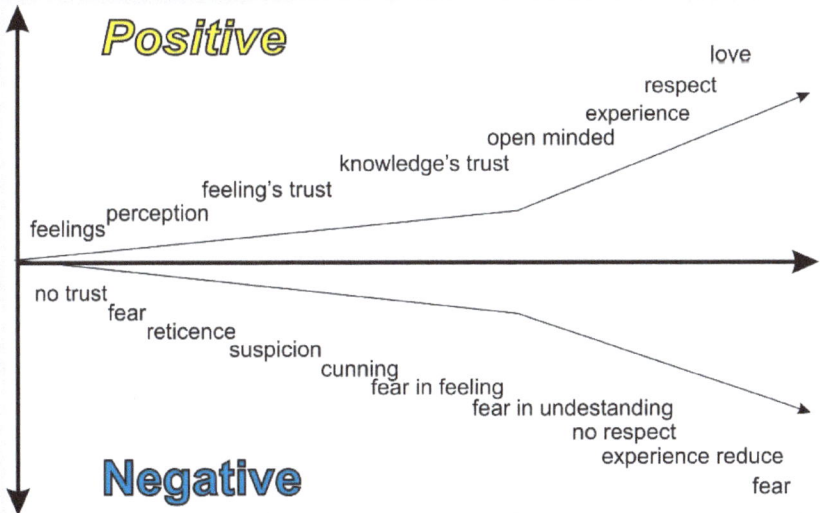

These pictures show a gradation of human development through its positive and negative thinking. What and where a person gets. The idea is that the awareness of importance and trust to your own feelings begins with heavy footsteps to gain experience. No experience is positive or negative. Human impressions can be positive or negative. Like the weather. There is no bad weather. The same way experience gives us new understanding. If we need to get that experience through the negative, it means that we do not want to get the knowledge through a pleasant experience and positive events. This is not always, but it is. Man gets negative and positive impressions of the results of his own actions, and with time he realizes, he can understand that a direction of thinking is changing in the direction of hopelessness, fear, and loss of sense of understanding.

I will remind you, or will show a good example about children's desire to understand. A child is sitting in front of fireplace watching it. It becomes interesting for him to understand what the fire is. He begins to approach his hand to the fire to try. Mother or grandmother, or someone from the family is watching this picture and is beginning to scold the child not to do so. The child becomes frightened and even more interested, because he wants it personally experience what it is. At first, the child may be afraid, but when he has a strong desire to reach the goal of understanding, he will be hard to try to reach the goal. They will try to stop him, but in fact nothing will stop him. Then the relative, watching this picture, will get tired and will decide to allow the child to try the bitter truth of life. He takes his little hand and helps reach the fire. First impressions will be a lesson for the whole life as a reminder what fire is. At the same time, the child will get the pleasure of achieving the desired goal. This experience to understand the fire is achieved through negative impressions of feeling the effects of fire through the body. Such unpleasant feelings can be of electricity, falling from a tree or a bicycle. To fall from a car or a motorcycle on the move is even more risky. However, this understanding adds a man incentive to be careful and fear of losing his life, to damage health and so on. He is aware of such threats when feeling threats less, when experiencing damage to himself. It stimulates the human to be more careful with his own desires and actions.

There are many examples with human health, relationships, at work and at rest. You can imagine your life as a way of repelling from negative to positive impressions. When there is more negative and the person gets used to it, without trying to find a way towards understanding and restoring feelings, then he remains in the negative zone for long, until the negative becomes so large that the consequences would be disastrous, or all that will turn the person in the other direction.

A simple example can be taken in mathematics in primary school. 2 + 2 what will be result? The question is not complicated, but setting a goal of the question requires an adult to think and to ask, whether to look for understanding and answers, or you have nothing to encourage you do it! The answer may be different and you will always be right, because you want to get the answer to any question in the form, regardless of what it may actually be. Therefore, the answer depends on the desire to get it, and therefore the content of need for this. If the question can be ignored or postponed then it should be done, and when it is not really relevant, or can be ignored, then it is better to say that the answer to this question does not exist, because you do not want it to be...

If again to recall the construction of the house, every brick is placed next to the previous or following the previous one. The same in taking the stairs. It's just simple to imagine. You step to the next step, you can go in different ways, but the main task lies to take each step slowly one by one. And you get a good picture in which every step you take in your life overcomes by a sense of desires and needs to make a move. You feel the ability to do next step with your body and senses, you decide to walk and walking, as a child, you enjoy achieved goal. Each next step will make you skills, that is experience, confidence, determination, the best feelings and the ability to feel. Which in turn will give you respect and trust to senses and understanding. In complete harmony of understanding and sensations you will feel the love of your own achievements.

Conversely, if you do not trust your own feelings and are afraid of making a move, because the previous, or the very first was unsuccessful, then you do not trust your feelings and you doubt. Only some significant stimulus and need almost make you do and dare to take this step. You are reluctant to do it, afraid to feel something again, you do not trust received sensations and experiences again. If you stumble over this step somewhere because of your own fear, it will give you even worse reason to become a more closed, suspicious and even cunning man. You think that it should be so, but in reality you are only going in the direction of even worse negative and even of falling down the steps to change attitudes. Fear creates fear only to a certain limit of the capability to stand this fear in possible human volume. Once Solomon said to a man who wanted gold "You can't take more than you can". All you say and do makes sense, not only good content and appearance. As already mentioned, more than you know, you cannot ever say and do. Everything has its contents and it weighs more in terms of its content usage.

Imagine a person who is inside the person as in the robot. All possible means to obtain information are outside, all senses and observations bring you information you need. If you close them, like a blind, deaf, etc., then burden falls on additional sensations and they are improving. If not the lack of sensory organ, the man would just develop it. He can develop the sense of touch or sight, for example, but without need or organ dysfunction, he will not do this. This means that the body is used and does not receive proper attention to its maintenance and development. If the person loses all the senses, no more information is coming in. Let us ask ourselves whether a person can develop without feeling anything or fewer? If you don't feel at all, you can not develop, because there are no possible tools to use. If only partially, then respectively partial development will be the basis for the possible development of great opportunities, but if a man puts such a goal. It is worth remembering if.

Development of opportunities already goes to the second theme of the story, so I will again draw conclusions and summarize the main issues of the topic. For this I will show you again for the third time the same image.

Picture. Choice.

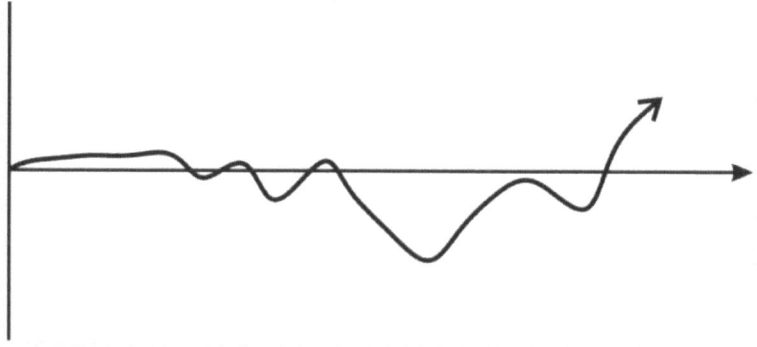

Man's way takes different directions to find the way to understanding, respect and love. He always has an opportunity of a choice, though the human destiny shows him the main and the only way – to make the next step with understanding, respect and love, otherwise the path will not create a better understanding and your home of understanding will never be built. Each brick of your understanding is a life step to understanding regardless what impressions you get from your own actions.

Is it so easy to self-develop and live?

I will repeat the question 'Is it so easy to self-develop and live?' It is worth after all the previous words to form an overall picture of your own understanding, or to summarize what was said. This can help to take the question into meaning parts of the common system.

It has so much been said and still a lot of things are left unsaid. As if the story is just beginning. Of course, I can say that knowing what we have next, having this experience, but I am constantly amazing feelings and impressions that continue. It is constantly developing thinking, and creating some notions after the sign "=", as in a task, gives us some conclusions. They do not have to be unique, and even true, they just have to be to start somewhere. That's why we'll just move on and enjoy the results of our thinking direction. To collect parts and to make a picture like a mosaic into one combined thing. Just do not rush and feel your understanding to make the picture more conscious than understandable.

So we should summarize general processes of human development and the development of its information. We can even omit a man as a creature. Here we are talking more about the information development with the help of something, but more complex and systemically bigger, better and more responsible. That is, the development of information in practice. Who may simply be information and at the same time be a subject with possibilities?! The human.

So let's generalize. Thinking as a basis of analysis depends on tools of body and soul, as energy to carry information. If it is difficult and you may not like it, then we can simply not be such scientific, technical and dry. We can decorate differently. The soul through the body feels more itself and the outer world. Man, as body and soul, enters the world of life and explores in practice possibilities and the outside world. Man learns to survive and can hardly reach understanding to develop, although consciously and subconsciously he is moving continually that way. Man is just not interested to live with the past, which does not already exist, and the unknown future ahead.

Let's take a look at the picture.

Picture. Time forms.

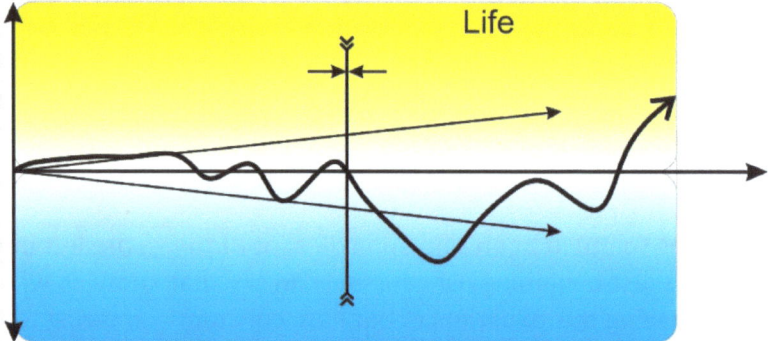

The picture shows us life movement along time period. The upper part reflects positive impressions and bottom in a dark color - negative. A man's life as an arrow goes from negative to positive and vice versa, choosing the direction of a lifetime.

The vertical line in the middle of the image with a mark inside shows the present time. Everything before this line shows the past and therefore everything after will be the future. All actions are pushing our experience and life in selecting the meaning of life because of its understanding. If understanding reduces or has a lot of hesitation, life will have a negative result. Seeking a way to ensure the necessary positive always comes up the question of understanding. When it does not increase, behavior content gets less until a person gets the negative so much to make him act more confidently to better understanding.

As in the example with a cat, which cornered. He makes his last attempt to escape, collecting all his strength. The same requires a large and significant event of loss of your health, family or other events that cause a person to simply disable his established thinking and to look at a problem or question radically with a goal to find a solution. Of course people are different and not everyone fits this scheme. Everyone has his own characteristics, which lead to his necessary actions and consequences. The man himself can trace his life and see what happens. For example, if you describe your actions verbally or in writing and outline them with exact expressions and values.

Let's look at another picture with a selection question.

Picture. Select.

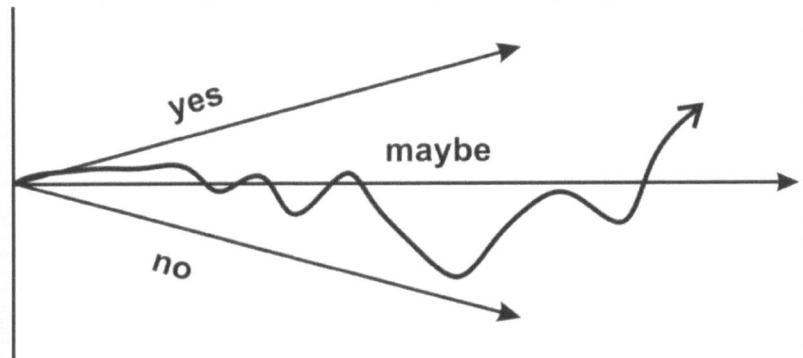

This picture has three components: the agreement "yes", hesitation "possible" and denial "no". What connection does it have with time? It's more a matter of choice. Time only allows you to change something and realize.

And it's more interesting not only to look, but to comment. It's really fun to make because of the practical awareness and soul acceptance of this understanding. When there comes any question people always have at least three possible answers: yes, no, maybe. What does this mean? No, I don't take it whatever reason and I definitely understand it and accept. That's good, if so, instead of saying "no" to emphasize the trend towards "yes", expressing uncertainty and intrigue. Therefore, when commenting the person's choice we should say that it is a question of literal decision without additional content.

Consequently, failure takes away an opportunity to take an interest in and have options because we refuse at once and it may be premature. When using uncertainty we lose time and it also does not lead us to understanding. During that time, you can choose to close a question of choice, or to discover and understand it. Answer "yes" gives more choice, more options and quality. The more a person agrees and chooses the better understands. Otherwise, it reduces the amount of choice having not tried to understand, and thus gets a sense of loss, it will always follow the person and he can not even understand it, as he closed the door and does not remember which.

For example, if you say that you do not want to study more in life or just say that you do not want to learn, then you choose a path that will not go in the direction of understanding and lead to more misunderstanding variant. The same will be with all your actions and consequences – more loss of understanding of what is happening. If you want to understand then you need to go in that direction, or to deceive yourself and to go in the opposite way. You can cancel your every decision, if you need to remember and cancel. You can pronounce it aloud or any other way to express it. Each solution pushes you to gain experience or time to prepare to take this experience.

Simply saying any solution of daily choices in any question will be searching variants of solution and understanding that will give you content, objectives and results. A negative decision will cut off the direction of thinking and life in general. Man needs time for any decision, but often the time delay only brings complications and consequences that have more negative value with moments of regret, frustration, misunderstanding and so on.

If you have a question: do you know this book, read, I recommend? The answer of negative direction without knowledge of the subject, that is the given book, blocks the way of understanding what it is and why it is offered. You can ask about the content and better read a few pages to close the question of understanding if this is exactly what you need. Understanding what a person does not like and does not need at this time is important to bring you closer to the desired, which is getting less distance. If you begin to doubt and delay, and then you can forget, not know and lose it. And the affirmative answer means to overcome your own reluctance, laziness, etc. and to meet the understanding. Everything happens at the right time. When we open a children's game puzzle with creating a picture of a boat with pieces, then we look for a suitable pattern. In practical life, a man constantly receives some particles of puzzle and even lose himself in them. How often do we have less willing to read, see or even understand?! Probably we have a lot of different questions like garbage piled up in the head, which we don't even remember what it is at all. But questions remain.

If you remove an excess flow of information, it becomes easier to sort out your own desires. It's like a lady cleaning the floor, people are constantly changing and making left dirty. It can not be removed, because you need to stop the process and allow the floor to dry. If to bring the trash all the time, it will pollute. If garbage is not taken out, it will grow and there comes a question what is easier to find a new home or clean it out?! And the same in everything.

A matter of choice in the negative direction and the frequent use of objections will always lead in the direction of closing the doors for an opportunity to understand and feel. Indecision will delay time of uncertainty and of a large number of errors to be at the beginning of the choice and the need to go in the opposite direction. It's better to understand than to spend time and life. Better to have something to feel and understand. However, we can always use the given situation. Decision should be made to go in the direction of understanding, if you really need it at the moment, and you need to give up if you are not yet ready. You will have to make the choice, but you can wait if there are opportunities and needs.

Look at the picture carefully and as long as possible. I will comment.

Picture. Life 2.

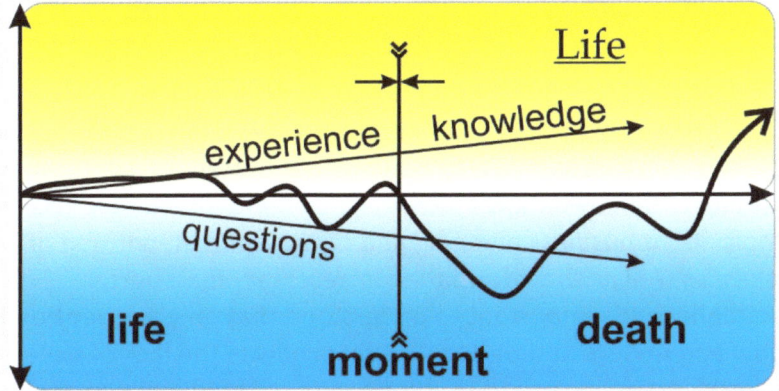

This picture better shows opportunity choices and consequences of understanding.

A question of choice in the positive direction gives us experience and an opportunity to see, wish and understand the needs. If we know, for example, how much money we have right now then it is easier to know, what we need and how much it will cost, as well as why we buy it.

Negative response increases the number of questions that pull a man down to the large number of errors, less understanding, less feeling and complete gradual decline of the meaning of life with the conclusion - death, in any sense. The increase of unsolved questions closes every next door to understanding and thus gives less number of answers. In the example with money we cannot count what we buy, if we have enough money and why we buy. Respectively, there will be even more questions that come to us at the checkout. And it may be that at the checkout, we will not have the funds at all... there are many answers as well as options, but they have one meaning - ignorance and not understanding of the unknown future as a consequence.

Human life in its present moment ask one question - what are we entering into the future with? If you clean around, calculate and determine your experience, mistakes, understanding of all that you know, this will help us to understand what to do next. We have already had an example with money. If we count the money then it is possible to know what we can expect for and where to go to. Experience and knowledge are also necessary to count as well as desires and dreams. Therefore, further I will repeat it again.

Knowing and understanding the lessons learned in the past, no matter which, it gives the opportunity to see the next step and realize opportunities in this present moment. If you worry about the unknown and do not go forward, learning how to do it better and safer, then the probability of deadly dangers increases. This was already mentioned in the topic about business planning and other topics. Repetition of mistakes, as well as the information is necessary for a better understanding. It's important to understand that only a repetition helps to know and understand better. The fear reflects the lack of necessary experience. Stepping into the future a man only reduces something unknown and incomprehensible that can inspire fear. Of course, if the person knows with what he is going in the future.

In the previous pictures of a human development around the circle, or in the key concepts system, terms of knowledge increase and expand. This is the ideal picture. There is no other way in human life, as the opportunity to meet his fear and understand it. This points to the many problems and misunderstandings that the person needs to understand in order to go to a better experience and to look at life differently.

The following image shows how a person is engaged in self-deception.

Picture. The realities of life.

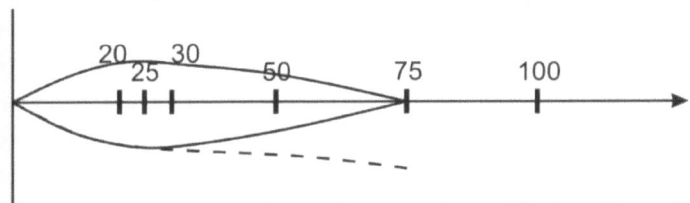

A man is approaching old age with body and soul, without developing any one of them. His desires, questions grow and pull him down if he does not give answers. Over time, a person says he has a lot of questions, but in fact most of them he has already got rid of, and they are rapidly reducing, reducing the path of the need in human life. The person gradually loses the questions and answers to understand. This has already been said enough about, the drawing only describes it better visually.

So, I can repeat the question again – is it so easy to self-develop?

You can drive all your lifetime and do not know how to turn around your car on a small platform. This surprised me and I've kept this example in mind for many years to understand it better with time.

Many people describe how to develop a sense of success, how to attract it, magnetize and so on. Feeling can be customized to meet specific goals and achieve its goal of becoming a successful and so forth. If you recall the popular topic of money and business, then just to make money can be quite easy, much more difficult is to develop yourself systematically. Has a person one question in life only? Does he have only a few such famous goals - money, family, child? This is like classes in school and years in human life. Man grows up and expands the range of needs, interests and abilities. The question is always the same if a person knows what he has and where he is going to?!

The answer to this question if human development can be such easy is clearly – no. This is my personal attitude. If everything were so clear and simple, and this lecture would not exist. I would not have to devote a lot of years for a better understanding and formation of this experience. I can add more, the less developed people, the more they kill, and people with a qualitatively different experience inclusively. The fear of the unknown frightens until it becomes known. Many scientists have been eliminated for this reason, and as others. Therefore, the experience is often necessary to hide, because it's much easier to destroy than to create.

Also it is worth noting the problem of the majority of people attitude to the minority of people with great possibilities of thinking, and so on. Each individual feels and understand differently about the question of development. How can we explain something unknown?

Does self-development have its end?

Here we come to the last significant item of this lecture. This has already actually been said many about, but maybe I haven't explained how it happens and if it is practically possible at all. There are many details and I cannot say them in one book, and certainly in one lecture. Remind yourself of the development's system of human knowledge, deepening the experience in each issue separately. That is, each simple question has many sub-questions and new details again. Layering of our practical knowledge happens this way as well as the depth formation of experience. Like a brick placed one after the other and each following circle of climbing up to the completion of construction.

Remember development round a circle, as well as the construction of the same house that it can be stopped on each masonry circle any time. But if actually to give an example with a brick, then it is difficult to imagine how one can make a new masonry at the same height. Therefore, let's remember a thinking process in solving any problem in mathematics. If the answer is incorrect, how is it possible to find out correct or not correct? Calculate again and again. The processes occur over and over again as long as there's no mistake. Much easier to imagine playing music in the player. Can we reverse it again? Sure we can and it does not surprise anyone, but just imagine for a while if you do not understand some question of your life you will just walk in a circle over and over again until you understand and cross it. This allows us to meet such errors again and not once.

So, we can understand that our experience increases or decreases, regardless of whether we pay our attention to this. Maybe it sounds silly, but it's easy to understand and it will be shown on the picture, and it has already been said more than once.

Let's go ahead and remind ourselves components of human life. Look at the picture.

Picture. Human connection.

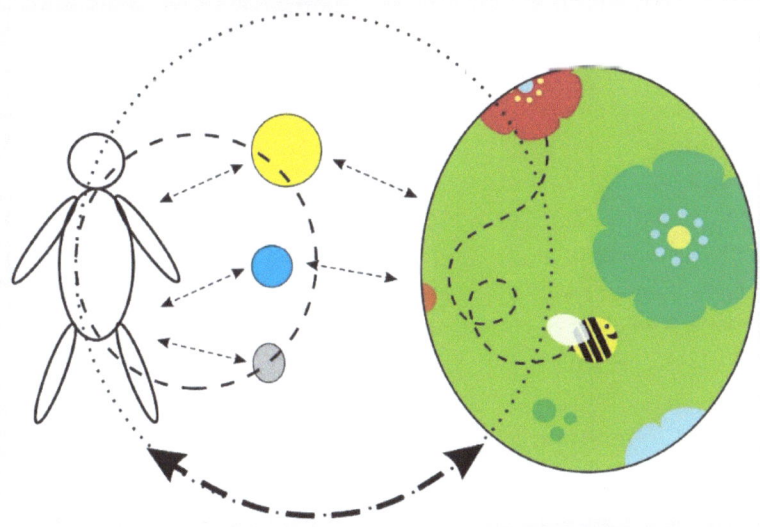

On the left side we can see a man and on the right – the environment in the form of land, eggs or else. In the middle of the picture we can observe not sun planets, but different means and instruments made by a man: books, magazines, expensive information tools, business objects, mountains, sea, oceans, trees, people.

A man communicates with the environment directly or with the help of other people's knowledge and tips.

This is as to understand the meaning of the story through a form of language and meaning of words. The same can be difficult sometimes to interpret from one language to another. How can you make a computer understand the human?!

Man explores the world through the established experience and opportunities somehow describe and explain it. In fact, everything in this world either directly or not interact between itself. If the man gains experience and sees the world only through the knowledge of other people or other means, he may lose and loses touch with the world. We have already mentioned constitution of a man. Our world forms from the smallest particle. Particle-to-particle creates a system. From simple systems to complex and very complex. Someone says he does not believe in God or the soul. The same you can do with the light and electricity. One can see the light every day and it's ok. If there were no electricity, it would certainly be a miracle to see such first. However, we already have it. The soul is only the energy system in conjunction with other layers of energy that form the human body. It is necessary first to determine what means the soul and then to enter some parameters in the word. What is God? You can believe or not. Nobody forbids. As long as you do not know and do not have any answers to a simple understanding of the structure of the body and the world in general, then what can we talk about God or things like that!? I liked the last book on the subject of the soul and afterlife by a hypnotherapist Michael Newton's "Journey of the soul". It describes the world of life on another level of existence. When we are professionals in a certain area, then it becomes a different world to others, which is necessary to understand, to make any conclusions, especially with professional authority.

That's why I started this topic with components of the relationship between man and world, to indicate the components and put them on the basis of the question. What does it mean "to believe" and "not to believe"? You can believe in anything, but if to put a question of knowledge about it then you may say you do not know or you do know. Put "believe" on the side of the future as unknown, as the question that you need to answer. Put the word "know" on the side of the past as something that you already know.

For example, we know how much money we have in our wallet. We know the exact number. We need not believe it, we do not steal the unknown. And if to ask you how much you can earn over the next year? You can say that you believe in the opportunity to earn a certain amount, or approximately, but you do not know exactly. Even when you know it, the matter is that the future is always unknown and it is not necessary to know it, because you can not change anything. Knowledge of the future allows us only to be aware of possible events. To change it allows knowledge of the past, which directly forms our present, our actions and abilities of understanding what we have, what we want and what we aspire to, and respectively, we are going that direction and will get there. Therefore it is necessary first to understand the past to know what may happen in the future.

A man has two important questions in his life: create or destroy. To give birth or to kill. And the most important thing is to know or not to know. Look at the following picture.

Picture. Age.

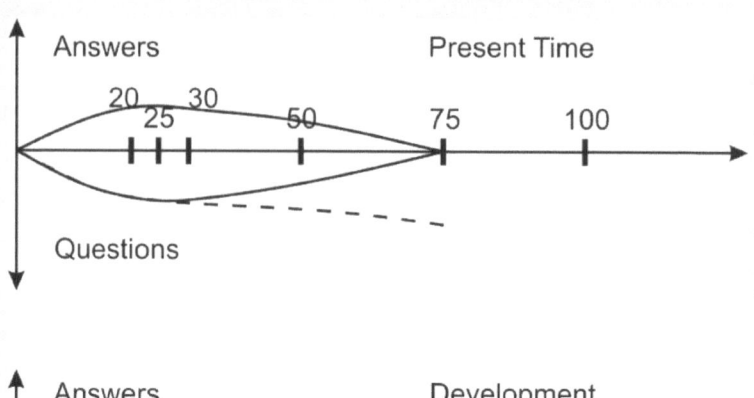

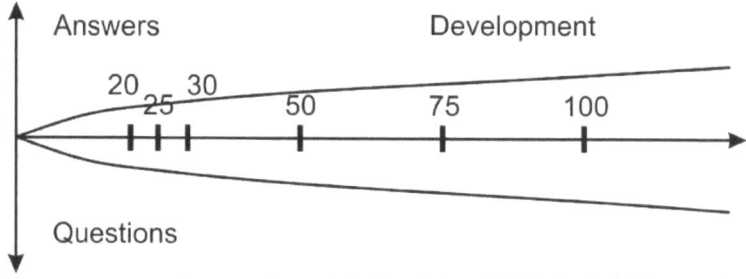

Picture title is "age". This picture shows better the contents of understanding – to develop and regress, to build and destroy, to make life and kill. Each man lives with these important questions almost every day. Every day he puts questions to understand and to do something, or something make worth and break, and then to be sorry for what done.

The upper part of the picture is already known. It shows the reality of the present. Man lives about hundred years. Dying at an average age of 75 years. The development of thinking occurs between the age of 30 years, let's can take it 25 years. After this age, people gradually reduce the number of questions and increase the lack of knowledge, the direction of thinking and its development.

So, a person intensively develops thinking till the age of 25 years. After completion of the physical development, the person stops to develop important - thinking, without considering it as a conscious understanding and component of development. Falling of interest and development continues slowly to the point when questions disappear and answers can no longer appear. Perhaps it is difficult to understand, but if to take it as task components, what has already been done, the understanding comes pretty quickly.

We can reduce them to simple values: known and unknown. If the unknown gets more, then the known gets closed. As well as not to use some muscle groups, they will atrophy. Everything without necessity dies. It is not a secret. That's why you can know or you can not.

Now, again, let us remember the pyramid, spiral development, system and even the bricks. All increases. Development proceeds from one quality to another. Questions replace other questions in depth. This picture with its lower part clearly demonstrate it. Development starts slowly from 25 years but surely. This happens only with visible results of person's conscious understanding. The man himself will not be somehow different, although the experience is difficult to hide. He is changing physically and especially mentally, psychologically. This is not an easy path. Just as in the example, when a person gets a job and while he has not learned to do his job, he will not know it at the proper level. When he finds out, he will understand the scheme and details of the work. It will be easy for him. The same is with development. But the question is, when does development and adult life in this style start? Perhaps many will be wondering what differs a person taking this path?!

What differs a person with a view to self-development? To notice such a man among others is rather difficult and to understand his life's details it is sometimes also difficult and unclear, but they are. The answer becomes quite simple. Imagine the development of the body separately, the soul and its components separately? It is difficult, I know. No need to show all these details here. It will be a separate book and a separate lecture. Many of the details of human development cannot fit in the head and not be acceptable, but they are there and the man will not ever want to abandon this way of life, if he steps on his natural path, as to walk on two legs or four, to be healthy and sick and dead... The same is difficult to give up a way of wealthy life and beautiful things, or warm sun and a nice bed, warm water and delicious coffee, it's so hard to give up real life in development. So let's get to the first question.

When begins conscious life in the direction of development? Look again at the picture at the top, and find the transition points to a decrease of the rate of development. Let us take the age of 20 and 30 years. In twenty you have more questions and desire. In thirty desire is about to be changed with decrease of questions and decrease of desire to search for answers. Then a man tries to make experience of survival in society and to set up life style. These points in 20 and 30 years are main and relevant.

You can feel your life conscious and rethink it at any age. Or you will achieve the same results as in young age, it is certainly a question of your desire and readiness. Everything can be quite difficult and you need to take this into account. It will not be so easy. Mostly not. However, this does not mean to lose faith and to think in a negative direction. Your any better conscious understanding will change you from inside at times. Unique experience feelings, which form you from inside. Therefore, it is important to feel the desire not to believe, and to inspect and investigate. You will change the format of thinking from survival to creation. These are completely different things, and closer to God and Love with a capital letter. It is difficult to understand without experiencing it all deeply.

The name of the lecture "Human self-development. The Basics." indicates the basics not accidentally. This is just the basis like the alphabet, in order to begin the journey. This is not even the beginning of conscious life. Start begins with the moment as on the picture in 30 years, when you go to a conscious understanding of the direction of your life due to results of your understanding. This understanding and experience first you need to generate and summarize. You need to check and investigate.

Further details will be explained.

3- Completion of the seminar

Summary of the main theses of the seminar

As you can see in the last topics, the audience was not offered to make conclusions but was given an opportunity of self-awareness of each person in the audience. Now we shall summarize the basic concepts and theses of the seminar. We had 9 questions and a lot of notions inside.

What means the development?

We can interpret this word "development" in different ways, but let's agree how you name your ship, so it will float. In the same way it is necessary to determine the meaning and understanding of words. They are direct meaning of our lives.

Thus, the development has been said as – to expand, change the quality to a better quality. This word development means increasing the quality and quantity of the subject. To develop, improve and so on. I think a picture of an inverted pyramid shows it better, where development begins from a narrow top.

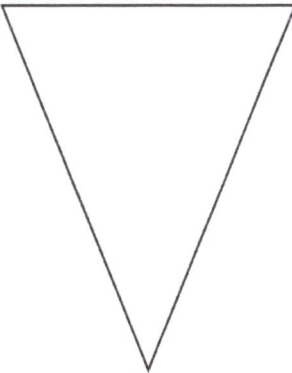

What is the purpose of any seminar?

This is the next question, and I liked most of all said that seminars are a collective means of educating people, better to say information transfer. It's difficult to add something more here, except you can only discuss in vain. But the main purpose of this topic is not a seminar as understanding, but the ability to see the experience through the seminar for self-determination. A man will have to teach himself alone, with a teacher, with the help of the teacher, with a book or even with a group of like-minded people. This is the basic idea of the topic.

How paints an artist a picture?

Good question and the picture will show again the answer better.

The artist has a finished drawing in his own head, and in front of himself he lays it down to separate parts and gradually forms, makes the image again together. This question is of professional relationship, as in this example of drawing. The same things does machinery mechanic, teacher or doctor. How much time do we all professionals have to learn to do these things in one activity sphere?! This is our life to learn how to take it apart and put it together in patience with time and professional attitude. This is the basic idea.

Development in business

Development questions in business are to bring one more example to the attention of the audience – business or professional activity. There were these words before:

Goals in business, as in personal life, are based on the ability to assume what – the goals –comprise, based on and whether they ever exist.

I think this statement fits better the given goal of understanding the topic. Business as understanding of what you have, what you can expect and plan accordingly. The better plan the better results. Results can help you plan better again...

Human development and its components.

Human development is a bit harder to characterize. I'll start with the already mentioned pyramid as a model, but with a system of life in which a person is born.

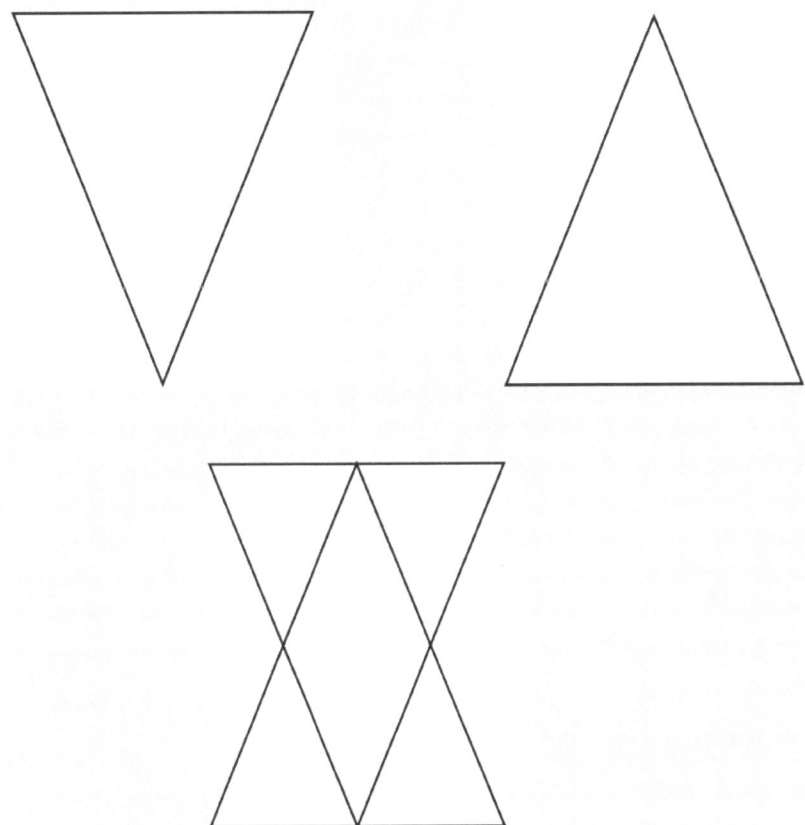

Pyramid of human development and system of life are combined into one image for the understanding of purpose and of human capabilities.

Best of all was said by these words.

Man from his birth deals with the ready environment and prepared information that he needs to take to pieces and learn. Anyway, the body and the environment push to it with the threat to human life. Everybody wants to live.

A man forms his knowledge systematically deepening into his study of the right questions. Man puts questions and finds answers. Later he uses the answers to create following questions in depth in hierarchy of the main question. That is, he puts sub-questions. Unnecessary and unsolved issues get lost over time and lose their meaning.

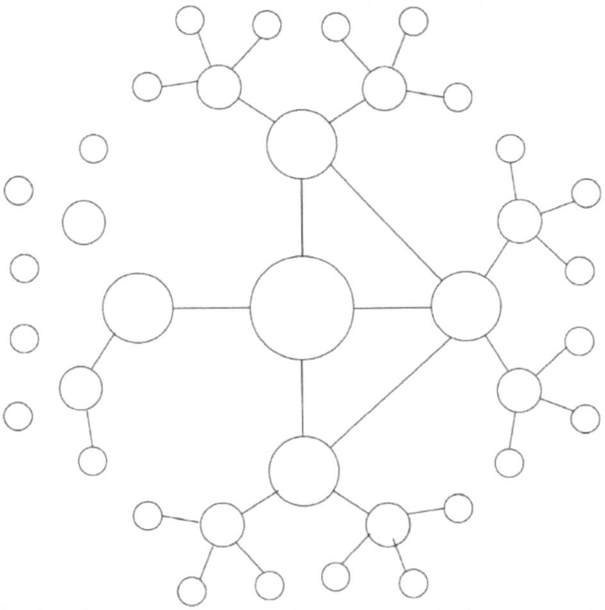

The following image shows the movement of a person in a spiral circle towards expanding his ability of thinking.

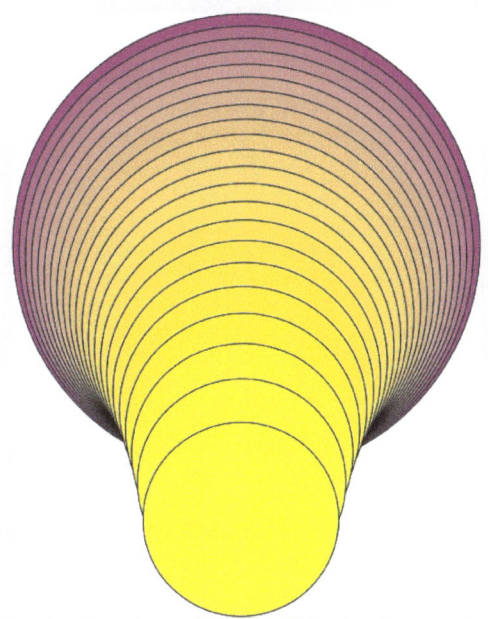

If unsolved questions don't let you move on, then you have to go round of one level and to look for missed questions. Errors are repeated and will be repeated, until you realize their relationship with the major related questions.

The following picture shows the components of system's life, that is the environment, and the human with his purpose including.

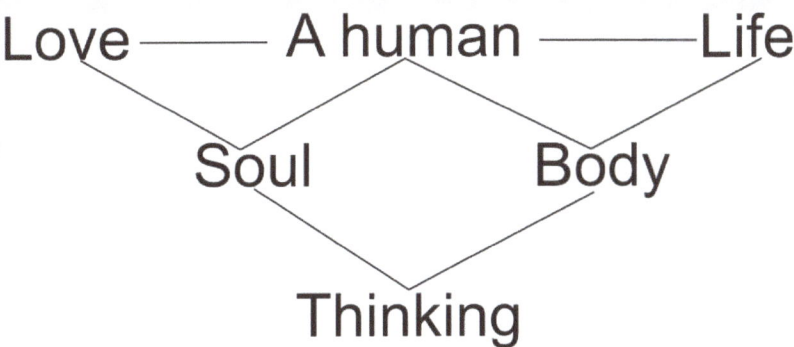

Stages of human development in the time interval

Stages of human development in the time interval are simple at this scale in the picture.

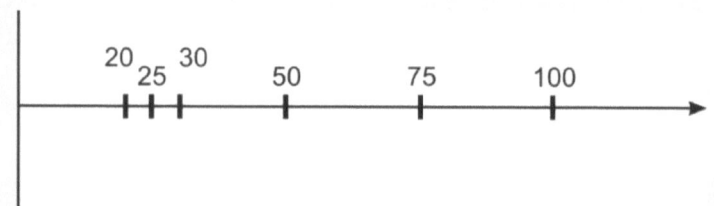

Take a look and find your time period to see your own achievements and understanding of your life. This picture only shows how, so to speak, professionally and responsibly we relate to our lives. And remember the stories about people who lived about 900 years and more!? Good stories. Think a bit, can it be casual that a man lives only 75 years!? What does he need to learn to think about?!

The following picture shows the variants and directions of human life. His wanders around and aspirations. Human way of life goes mainly through negative, because to learn to understand something, you need to try and this is largely done through mistakes. The question always remains whether a person wants to comprehend more to come in the positive part!? To understand not only how to become successful but to understand – life !?

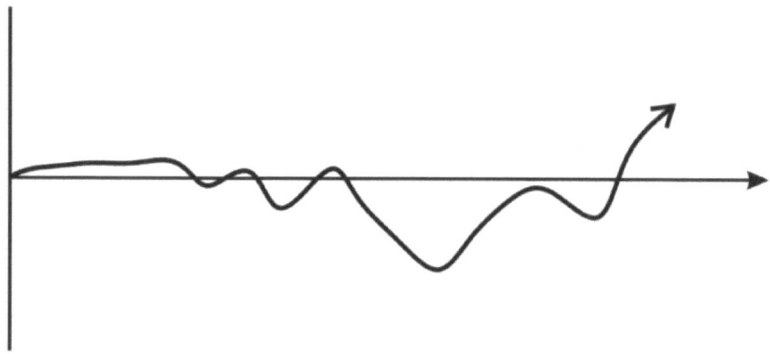

Table of negative and positive, its meaning

To understand life through negative and positive, as the human calls these impressions, is not an easy question. My favorite words on the subject are "How to measure human life and the human? What unit or concept should be selected as the basis? Give yourself an answer and tell me your thoughts out loud".

How to indicate life or the human, if you do not know the world in its components!

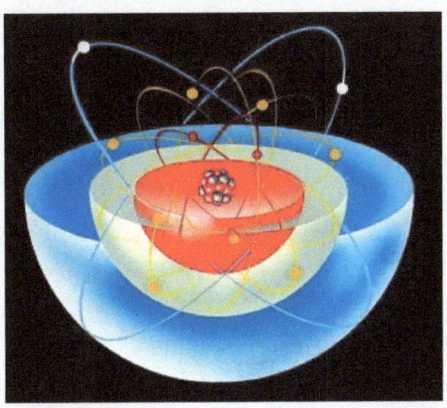

This way an atom was created, the same was the whole system of life in a simple structure with understanding of its structure's core. Each pyramid, as the law have the core, middle...

The lowest part of the world in the form of light creates our world at different levels. Earth and our common vision of the visible world is only the top of a very large iceberg. But if we remember that everything has a center, the same the man just copies life, shows and proves again the basis of understanding. Such as a computer. Information is transmitted through the light current and displayed on the monitor and in the actions. Experience is generated with information that people use, and what has already been mentioned. This is the basic idea of the topic.

Is it so easy to self-develop and live?

Is it that really easy for the person to do life or is he really so smart or sometimes he seems to be? If we turn back to previous topics, the answer will that he has inside his soul, his expertise. But this is possible only if the person has come to such understanding. What prevents this?

Matter of choice.

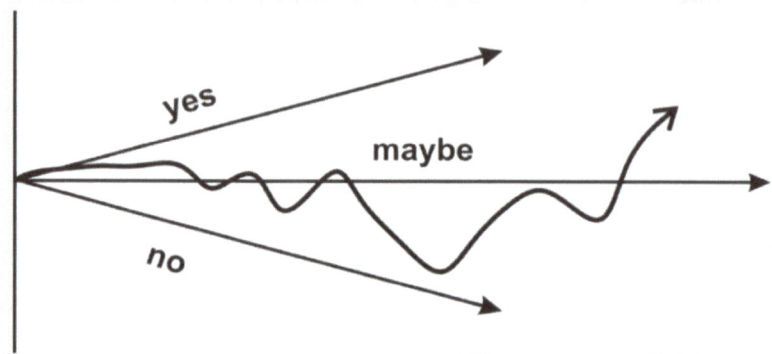

Matter of choice always gives us an opportunity and questions to open new comprehension or not still understand, to doubt, because of fear or other reason, or to give up and close the door to new experiences. In our expectations, or failure to understand something we lose this opportunity before the awareness of its need and return to the question again. Otherwise, the human one after one closes doors to better understanding and the way of life in development.

The following picture shows all the beauty of human choice and the results of such life.

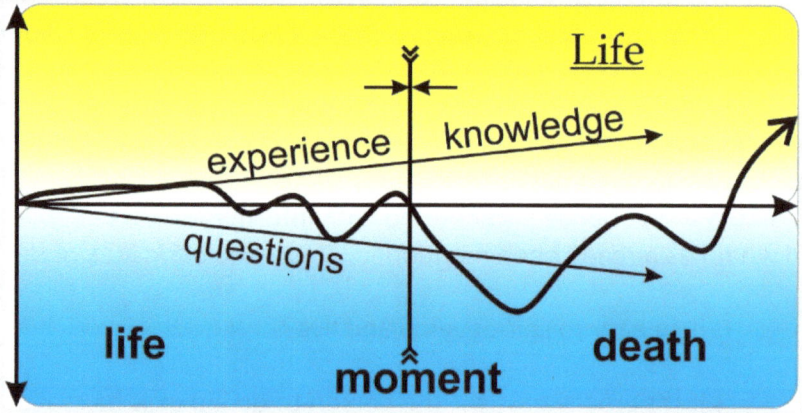

And this picture shows the reality, the level of self-deception and the age interval realities of human life. The human himself makes compress the limits of life, as to drive the cat in the corner, as it was in the example. Then try to look back and ask yourselves what is the price of your life?!

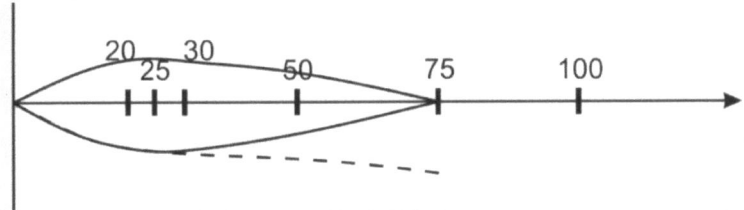

Does self-development have its end?

Good question and the answer, what is most interesting, has been mentioned not even once in different themes. But the following picture shows the known reality and real life in its consciousness, if to reduce the number of words.

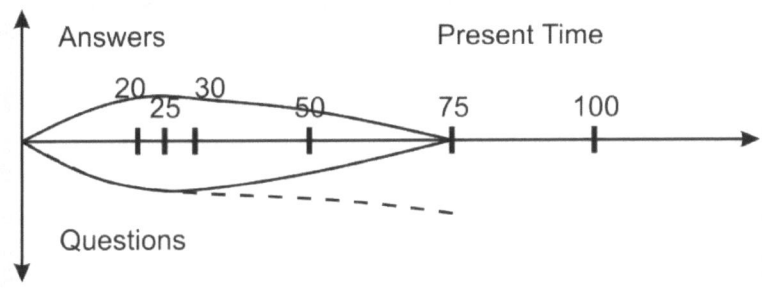

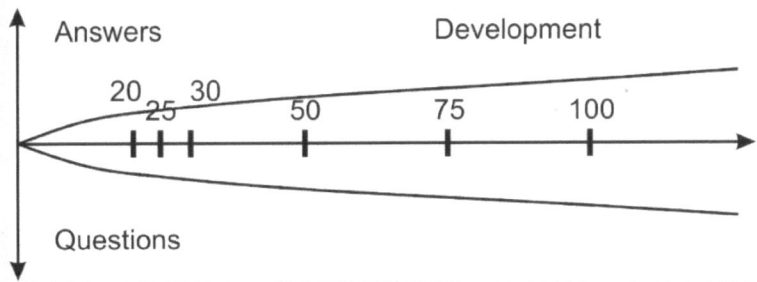

And you should still remember that a human and life communicate directly. If the human understands life exclusively through other people's experience, and does not check it, just believe and does not understand, does not know then the whole self-development will be within gained experience. As evidenced by the human understanding of the feeling of his body, food, rhythm of life, development opportunities and many other less or more important questions!?

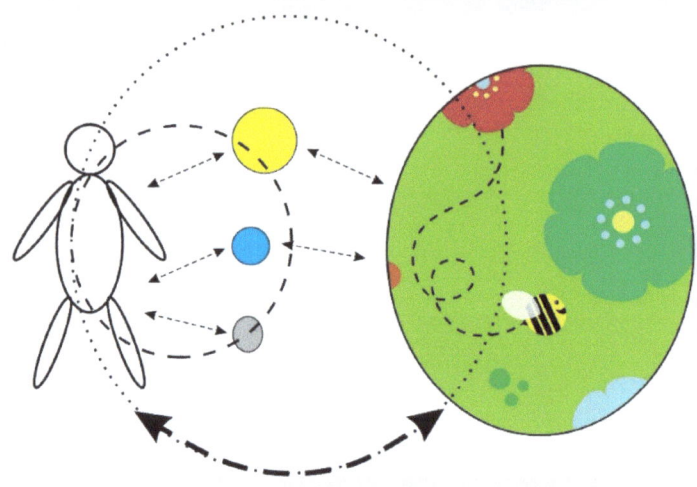

The audience poll about received basic knowledge

The most important task of the teacher or lecturer is to find out the quality and quantity of gained knowledge. The lecture can not teach much. Man has the ability to remember for a short time. Memorization process is based on individual personal priorities to get what he wants, and then satisfy his curiosity. The most people may have no need in the information, it will not justify their expectations etc. Moreover, people can block information that does not fit in their head and when they don't wish to believe and understand it, even though we are not talking about believing it all. This lecture is a data for the task that you need to understand and personally check in life to give some answers. In court, every person is trying to prove or disprove his involvement in the sentence. So everywhere.

Therefore, it'd be better to read the questions, quotes and theses of major themes in the previous topic "Summary of the main theses of the seminar". First answer yourself these questions with no hesitation, and please try to use as little words as you can. Answer please as short as possible, without thinking and remembering what was said. Next time alone you will be able to evaluate other way. If there is something not clear at all or partly, put questions to the author to repeat or explain.

The audience poll about questions for future consideration

The lecture is a general explanation of the basics. It cannot contain many more components on each question of human life and human being. These are separate issues and studied separately in depth. Fundamentals mean the beginning of the formation of consciousness, as it has been said from survival to development. Start of conscious development begins from the moment of its understanding.

So please put any questions that may be of interest human self-development to form the following lectures to explore life together.

I have to give an example, which is more than 10 years of its formation to fully understand it.

Two people drown themselves. Salvation variant 1. People save themselves separately. Question: What percentage of survival? Response – small and close to zero. Variant 2. One person rescue to save the other at the cost of his own life. The survival rate – 50 * 50. Variant 3. Two people come together for the common salvation. Percentage of survival – large and close to 100%.

The human, in my opinion, is on the way from variant 1 to 2, and only a small number of people already understand the importance of the transition from 2 to 3. This is just a thought, but your personal understanding and desire is more important. Your choice will be the most important and of each one separately, providing the basis for life.

So, let's develop together. We need everyone to each other. Development does not provide destruction. Every human life is of inestimable importance and of great value. Everyone, regardless of whether he is aware of it or not, needs in another person and should not harm him. To destroy others lives is not profitable and brings only the deterioration of society and the individual, destroys, regardless of whether he knows how it happens.

Please send me questions on the topics of interesting seminars and lectures to my e-mail stated at the beginning and at the end of the lecture.

Saying goodbye and the importance of knowledge to the authority

The lecture came to its end. Almost all scheduled was said. Lecture maybe is not perfect, but in fact, it should not be such. The most important task is to tell you desired content as clearly as possible. Not everyone can understand everything. Everyone needs time. It is enough. In this last topic I specified question authority.

Initially, the author introduced himself without specifying details of his individual. The importance of this lecture is inside the experience, in the information reported, and in no case the population of the author or the imposition of thoughts.

If someone is not satisfied with the information provided, then consider it prudent and incredibly interesting theory, certainly not related to reality. It's your attitude, your choice and your understanding. When something changes, you are always welcome again.

Those who are interested in information about life and human development can go for help with any questions to the author or the project. Project BM Love and Life at the moment is planned as a development of the school of personality development.

Grateful to all for your understanding, support and any help in development program of the project.

I love you, appreciate and understand. You are always welcome on the road of joint development.

Goodbye.

Contacts

Project VM Love And Life school
vmloveandlife@gmail.com
Author: Mykola V.
Ukraine , 2015

Love

&

Life

About the Book
The book reflects the results of studies of more than 15 years. Areas of research are the psychology of life in general and human life through his body physiology, psychology, soul, energy, human rights and peace, content protection and rights, yoga, nutrition, healthy lifestyle, business, the issue of self-development. Research continues. The purpose of the book is to ask a human to live with understanding, consciousness or in chaos, and invite everyone to join. The purpose of research - life through love, respect and understanding in the practical usage and database creation of experience for documentation and to transfer information to other people and to future generations.

About the Author
The author explores the life from a childhood. He began to think of writing books in ninth grade. What am I going to write when I do not know anything? I can write something, but it will not make sense. Since then he began research work on the study of human life. The author has experience as a teacher of foreign languages, translator of foreign languages, sales manager, businessman, he practiced psychological counseling, massage, yoga, energy, a diary writing, articles, poems and small stories writing. Author explored various spheres of human activity and behavior parallel. All it took more than 15 years of life.

2015

www.ingramcontent.com/pod-product-compliance
Lightning Source LLC
Chambersburg PA
CBHW050808290526
45792CB00001B/32